Contents

Introduction

This series of books is intended to support the continuing growth and development of independent learning and practical activities, which are key features of the Early Years Foundation Stage.

Children in Key Stage One need and deserve the chance to build on the best of practice in the Early Years Foundation Stage, which carefully balances adult directed tasks with learning that children initiate and develop themselves, often in the company of responsive adults. These activities, which include sand and water play, construction, role play, independent mark making and writing, creative work, dance and movement, and outdoor play, are some of the activities children value most and miss most in Years One and Two.

> Parent: 'What's it like in Year 1?'
>
> Child: 'There en't no sand and the work's too 'ard.'

This quote from a Year 1 boy echoes the feelings of many children who need to continue the learning styles and situations offered in Reception classes. However, many teachers in Key Stage One feel intense pressure to concentrate on activities that require recording and increasing levels of direction by adults. Why is this, and is it right for teachers to feel so pressured?

One thing we know from research is that practical activity and independent learning are essential for brain growth and reinforcement of growing abilities throughout childhood, at least till the onset of puberty, and for many children this is a lifelong need. We also know that the embedding of learning and the transformation of this into real understanding takes time and practice. Skills need to be reinforced by revisiting them in many different contexts in child initiaed learning, and practical challenges, and practical tasks in real life situations will be far more effective than rote learning, worksheets or adult direction.

> 'I hear and I forget,
>
> I see and I remember,
>
> I do and I understand.'
>
> Ancient Chinese Proverb

EVERY CHILD MATTERS

The five outcomes:

Enjoy and achieve

Stay safe

Be healthy

Make a positive contribution

Achieve economic well-being

It is also clear from brain research that many boys (and some girls) are just not ready by the end of Reception to embark on a formal curriculum which involves a lot of sitting down, listening and writing. Their bodies and their brains still need action, challenge and freedom to explore materials and resources in freedom.

But this does not mean that challenge should be absent from such activity! The brain feeds on challenge and novelty, so teachers and other adults working in Key Stage One need to structure the experiences, so they build on existing skills and previous activities, while presenting new opportunities to explore familiar materials in new and exciting ways. Such challenges and activities can:

- be led by the Programme of Study for Key Stage One;
- focus on thinking skills and personal capabilities;
- relate to real world situations and stimuli;
- help children to achieve the five outcomes for Every Child Matters.

In Carrying on in Key Stage 1, we aim to give you the rationale, the process and the confidence to continue a practical, child centred curriculum which also helps you as teachers to recognise the requirements of the statutory curriculum for Key Stage One. Each book in the series follows the same format, and addresses objectives from many areas of the National Curriculum. Of course, when children work on practical challenges, curriculum elements become intertwined, and many will be going on simultaneously.

The Role of the Adult

Of course, even during child initiated learning, the role of the adult is crucial. Sensitive adults play many roles as they support, challenge and engage the children in their care. High quality teaching is not easy! If teachers want to expand experiences and enhance learning, they need to be able to stand back, to work alongside, and extend or scaffold the children's learning by offering provocations and challenges to their thinking and activity. The diagram below attempts to describe this complex task, and the way that adults move around the elements in the circle of learning. For ease of reading we have described the elements in the following way, and each double page spread covers all three of the vital roles adults play.

Recognising and building on the practical activities which children have experienced before

This element of the process is vital in scaffolding children's learning so it makes sense to them. Your knowledge of the Foundation Stage curriculum and the way it is organised will be vital in knowing where to start. Teachers and other adults should have first hand knowledge of both the resources and the activities which have been available and how they have been offered in both child initiated and adult led activities. This knowledge should be gained by visiting the Reception classes in action, and by talking to adults and children as they work. Looking at Reception planning will also help.

Understanding the range of adult roles, and the effect different roles have on children's learning

Responsive adults react in different ways to what they see and hear during the day. This knowledge will influence the way they plan for further experiences which meet emerging needs and build on individual interests. The diagram illustrates the complex and interlinking ways in which adults interact with children's learning. Observing, co-playing and extending learning often happen simultaneously, flexibly and sometime unconsciously. It is only when we reflect on our work with children that we realise what a complex and skilled activity is going on.

Offering challenges and provocations

As the adults collect information about the learning, they begin to see how they can help children to extend and scaffold their thinking and learning. The adults offer challenges or provocations which act like grit in an oyster, provoking the children to produce responses and think in new ways about what they know and can do.

Linking the learning with the skills and content of the curriculum

As the children grapple with new concepts and skills, adults can make direct links with curriculum intentions and content. These links can be mapped out across the range of knowledge, skills and understanding contained in the curriculum guidance for Key Stage One. It is also possible to map the development of thinking skills, personal capabilities and concepts which link the taught curriculum with the real world.

The adult as extender of learning
discusses ideas
shares thinking
makes new possibilities evident
instigates new opportunities for learning
extends and builds on learning and interests
supports children in making links in learning
models new skills and techniques

The adult as co-player
shares responsibility with the child
offers suggestions
asks open questions
responds sensitively
models and imitates
plays alongside

The adult as observer
listens attentively
observes carefully
records professionally
interprets skilfully

Looking for the Learning

As children plan, explore, invent, extend, construct, discuss, question and predict in the rich experiences planned and offered, they will communicate what they are learning through speech and actions, as well as through the outcomes of activities. Assessment for learning involves adults and children in discussing and analysing what they discover. Reflecting on learning, through discussion with other children and adults, is a key factor in securing skills and abilities, fixing and 'hard wiring' the learning in each child's brain. And, of course, teachers and other adults need to recognise, confirm and record children's achievements, both for the self esteem this brings to the children and to fulfil their own duties as educators.

You could find out what children already know and have experienced by:

* talking to them as individuals and in small groups;
* talking to parents and other adults who know them well (teaching assistants are often wonderful sources of information about individual children);
* visiting the Reception classes and looking at spaces, storage and access to resources, including the use of these out of doors;
* providing free access to materials and equipment and watching how children use them when you are not giving any guidance;
* talking as a group or class about what children already know about the materials and those they particularly enjoy using.

Using the curriculum grid to observe, to recognise learning and celebrate achievement

At the end of each section you will find a curriculum grid which covers the whole Programme of Study for Key Stage 1. This is a 'shorthand version' of the full grid included at the end of the book on pages 69-74. A black and white photocopiable version of the grid appears on page 8, so you can make your own copies for planning and particularly for recording observations.

We suggest that as the children work on the provocations and other challenges in this book, adults (teachers and teaching assistants) can use the grid to observe groups of children and record the areas of the curriculum they are covering in their work. The grids can also be used to record what children say and describe in plenary sessions and other discussions.

These observations will enable you to recognise the learning that happens as children explore the materials and engage with the challenging questions you ask and the problems you pose. And of course, as you observe, you will begin to see what needs to happen next; identifying the next steps in learning! This logical and vital stage in the process may identify:

* some children who will be ready for more of the same activity;
* some who need to repeat and reinforce previous stages;
* some who need to relate skills to new contexts, the same activity or skill practiced in a new place or situation;
* some who will want to extend or sustain the current activity in time, space or detail;
* others who will wish to record their work in photos, drawings, models, stories, video etc.

Critical and Thinking Skills

The grid also identifies the key skills which children need for thinking about and evaluating their work. Many schools now observe and evaluate how well these skills are developing when children work on challenging projects and investigations.

"**Sand** is somewhere between stone and earth. It can be compressed hard and yet it can become fluid. It has a sense of strength, fragility and movement."
Andy Goldsworthy
Sculptor

Taking it Further

Offering extension activities is a way of scaffolding children's learning, taking the known into the unknown, the familiar into the new, the secure into the challenging. It is the role of the adult to turn their knowledge of the children into worthwhile, long term lines of enquiry and development which will become self-sustaining and last throughout life.

At the end of each section in the book you will find a selection of useful resources, links and other information to help you bring construction to life. You could use these resources by encouraging individuals and groups:

* to **use the Internet** to find images and information;

* to **use ICT equipment** such as cameras, tape recorders, video and dictaphones to record their explorations and experiments;

* to **explore information books** in libraries and other places at home and at school;

* to **make contact by email and letter** with experts, craftsmen, artists, manufacturers, suppliers and other contacts;

* to **make books, films, PowerPoint presentations**;

* to **record their work** in photographs and other media;

* to **respond to stimluli** such as photographs, video, exhibitions and other creative stimuli;

* to **look at the built and natural environment** with curiosity, interest and creativity;

* to **become involved in preserving the natural world**, develop environmental awareness and support recycling;

* to **look at the world of work** and extend their ideas of what they might become and how they might live their lives;

* to **develop a sense of economic awareness** and the world of work in its widest sense;

* to **feel a sense of community** and to explore how they might make a contribution to the school and wider communities in which they live;

* to **work together and develop the ability to think, reason and solve problems** in their learning.

We recommend that younger children should always work with an adult when accessing search engines and Internet sites.

The suggested resources include websites, books, contacts and addresses. There are also some photographs which may inspire young learners as they work on the provocations and challenges suggested.

We hope you will find the ideas in this book useful in stimulating your work with children in Year 1 and Year 2. The ideas, photos and provocations we have included are only a start to your thinking and exploring together, of course you and the children will have many more as you start to expand the work they do in these practical areas, providing a rich curriculum base using familiar and well loved materials.

Ros Bayley, Lynn Broadbent, Sally Featherstone: 2007

Literacy

	Lit 1 speak	Lit 2 listen	Lit 3 group	Lit 4 drama	Lit 5 word	Lit 6 spell	Lit 7 text1	Lit 8 text2	Lit 9 text3	Lit10 text4	Lit11 sentence	Lit12 presentation
	1.1	2.1	3.1	4.1	5.1	6.1	7.1	8.1	9.1	10.1	11.1	12.1
	1.2	2.2	3.2	4.2	5.2	6.2	7.2	8.2	9.2	10.2	11.2	12.2

Numeracy

	Num 1 U&A	Num 2 count	Num 3 number	Num 4 calculate	Num 5 shape	Num 6 measure	Num 7 data
	1.1	2.1	3.1	4.1	5.1	6.1	7.1
	1.2	2.2	3.2	4.2	5.2	6.2	7.2

Date	
Names	

Science

	SC1 Enquiry			SC2 Life processes					SC3 Materials		SC4 Phys processes		
	Sc1.1	Sc1.2	Sc1.3	Sc2.1	Sc2.2	Sc2.3	Sc2.4	Sc2.5	Sc3.1	Sc3.2	Sc4.1	Sc4.2	Sc4.3
	1.1a	1.2a	1.3a	2.1a	2.2a	2.3a	2.4a	2.5a	3.1a	3.2a	4.1a	4.2a	4.3a
	1.1b	1.2b	1.3b	2.1b	2.2b	2.3b	2.4b	2.5b	3.1b	3.2b	4.1b	4.2b	4.3b
	1.1c	1.2c	1.3c	2.1c	2.2c	2.3c		2.5c	3.1c		4.1c	4.2c	4.3c
	1.1d				2.2d				3.1d				4.3d
					2.2e								
					2.2f								
					2.2g								

ICT

	ICT 1 finding out		ICT 2 ideas	ICT 3 reviewing	ICT 4 breadth
	1.1a	1.2a	2a	3a	4a
	1.1b	1.2b	2b	3b	4b
	1.1c	`1.2c	2c	3c	4c
		1.2d			

PE

	PE1 devel skills	PE2 apply skills	PE3 evaluate	PE4 fitness	PE5 breadth
	1a	2a	3a	4a	5a dance
	1b	2b	3b	4b	5b games
		2c	3c		5c gym

History

	H1 chronology	H2 events, people	H3 interpret	H4 enquire	H5 org & comm	H6 breadth
	1a	2a	3a	4a	5a	6a
	1b	2b		4b		6b
						6c
						6d

Geography

	G1.1 & G1.2 enquiry		G2 places	G3 processes	G4 environment	G5 breadth
	1.1a	1.2a	2a	3a	4a	5a
	1.1b	1.2b	2b	3b	4b	5b
	1.1c	1.2c	2c			5c
	1.1d	1.2d	2d			5d
			2e			

Art & Design

	A&D1 ideas	A&D2 making	A&D3 evaluating	A&D4 materials	A&D5 breadth
	1a	2a	3a	4a	5a
	1b	2b	3b	4b	5b
		2c		4c	5c
					5d

PHSE & C

	PSHEC1 conf & resp	PSHEC2 citizenship	PSHEC3 health	PSHEC4 relationships
	1a	2a	3a	4a
	1b	2b	3b	4b
	1c	2c	3c	4c
	1d	2d	3d	4d
	1e	2e	3e	4e
		2f	3f	
		2g	3g	
		2h		

D&T

	D&T 1 developing	D&T 2 tool use	D&T 3 evaluating	D&T 4 materials	D&T 5 breadth
	1a	2a	3a	4a	5a
	1b	2b	3b	4b	5b
	1c	2c			5c
	1d	2d			
	1e	2e			

Music

	M1 performing	M2 composing	M3 appraising	M4 listening	M5 breadth
	1a	2a	3a	4a	5a
	1b	2b	3b	4b	5b
	1c			4c	5c
					5d

Critical Skills	Thinking Skills
problem solving	observing
decision making	classifying
critical thinking	prediction
creative thinking	making inferences
communication	problem solving
organisation	drawing conclusions
management	
leadership	

Notes on how to take the learning forward:

Key to KS1 PoS on Pages 69-74

Funnels, tubes and scoops

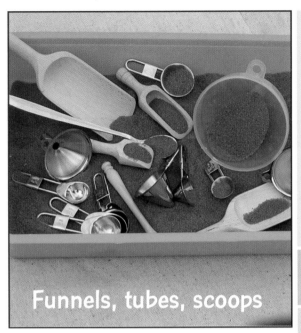

Funnels, tubes, scoops

Previous experience in the Foundation Stage

Children will have had experience of simple scoops and funnels in the Foundation Stage and even before. They are classic sand tools for:

* free play in sand trays and boxes indoors and in the garden;
* scooping sand into containers;
* lifting sand and letting it fall, exploring how it moves;
* filling and emptying diggers and boats;
* filling bottles and other containers with narrow necks;
* ladling sand into paper or plastic bags in role play, as 'food' or 'shopping';
* carrying sand around in buckets and barrows.

Pause for thought

In the early stages of working with these materials it is crucial to continue to observe the children. Only by doing this can you set developmentally appropriate challenges and provocations. The ideas listed here are offered as suggestions; the most exciting challenges will arise from children's own interests and motivations, which will only become apparent as you spend time with them, watching and joining them in their play. As you do this, you will be moving between the three interconnecting roles of observer, co-player, extender described below, and will be able to decide what you need to do next to take the learning forward.

The responsive adult (see page 5)

In three interconnecting roles, the responsive adult will be:

* observing
* listening
* interpreting

observer

* **modelling**
* **playing alongside**
* **offering suggestions**
* **responding sensitively**
* **initiating with care!**

co-player

* discussing ideas
* sharing thinking
* modelling new skills
* asking open questions
* being an informed extender
* instigating ideas & thoughts
* supporting children as they make links in learning
* making possibilities evident
* introducing new ideas and resources
* offering challenges and provocations

extender

Offering challenges and provocations - some ideas:

As children get older they can manage much smaller versions of the tools they have been using in the Foundation Stage. Search in bargain shops, cook shops, and garden centres for small versions of scoops, funnels, measuring spoons, and look for smaller containers to pour and scoop into. Add some small bottles, funnels and tubing, and this activity will help to refine fine motor skills for writing and 3D vision for reading.

? Find a way to tell which scoop holds the most sand. How did you do it?

? Use the biggest scoop to fill the biggest container. How many scoops did it need? Now use the biggest scoop and the smallest container. How many did it need? Try the smallest scoop and the biggest container.

? Fix one of the funnels into the end of one of the tubes. Now see how well it works. Try other combinations of tubes, funnels and scoops to find out which ones work best with different containers.

? Can you find a way of suspending a funnel and tube so you don't have to hold it while you pour in the sand. How did you do it?

? Experiment with dry and damp sand. Which works best with the scoops? ... with the tubes? ... with the funnels? Why do you think this is?

? Find a way of testing all the scoops so you can find out which one holds most sand. How did you do it? Were there any surprises?

? Look at some recycled bottles and other containers. Can you make your own scoops from these? Try some bottles with handles (from milk or juice) and make these into scoops by cutting away the bits of the bottle that you don't need. Take care with cutting tools!

? Find a really big container and fill it with sand, using your scoops. Can you find out how heavy the container is?

Ready for more?

- ✋ Set up a challenge with your friends. Agree on a container and a scoop or spoon. Now each one guesses how many scoops will fill the container. Record the guesses, and then measure. Who was nearest? Try again with a different container.

- ✋ Use scoops, funnels and tubing to transfer the sand from one sand box to another without touching the sand. How did you do it? Try with wet and dry sand - which is easiest?

- ✋ Can you use scoops and funnels to make a sand wheel work? Could you design a different sand machine, and make it with boxes, tubes and glue?

- ✋ Dry sand goes through tubes and funnels more easily than damp sand. How can you turn damp sand into dry sand? Do some experiments with your ideas and record what you find out in photos or a chart.

- ✋ Find some construction gears, straws or other pieces to make sand machines with scoops on them. Use the machines to shift the sand or load lorries and trucks.

- ✋ Look at the big sand pit machine on this page. How does the sand get up the conveyor belt? Could you make a machine to lift sand up so you can make piles or load toy lorries?

Materials, equipment suppliers, websites, books and other references

Suppliers of scoops, shovels and other sand toys:
For beach and sand toys including diggers and shovels and a ride on digger: www.growingtreetoys.com
ASCO Educational; suppliers of equipment and tools for sand play: www.ascoeducational.co.uk for sand trays, scoops and tools
Other education suppliers will have more equipment, try;
Eduzone: www.eduzone.co.uk
Hope: www.hope-education.co.uk
Early Learning Centre: www.elc.co.uk
TTS Group have a wide range of diggers and other sand toys: www.tts-group.co.uk
Get silver sand from an educational supplier or garden centre - builder's sand is very gritty and sometimes stains hands and clothes. Bags of gravel and pebbles from garden centres are a cheap way of extending resources for digging and scooping.

For images of scooping and pouring try Google Images. Just enter a word of something you want to see, and pictures will appear ('digger' 'scoop' 'sand' 'seaside' 'sandcastle' 'sand wheel' etc).

Try The Building Centre www.buildingcentre.org.uk go to 'links/education' and find the school of architecture nearest to you. they might be interested in working with the children on a project using some of the ideas in this book!
Some suitable books for younger readers include:
Sand and Water Play: Simple, Creative Activities for Young Children; Sherrie West; Gryphon House
The Little Book of Sand and Water; Sally Featherstone; A&C Black
Sand and Soil (Rocks, Minerals, and Resources); Beth Gurney; Crabtree Publishing
Wild About Trucks and Diggers; Caroline Bingham; Ticktock media.

Curriculum coverage grid overleaf

Potential NC KS1 Curriculum Coverage through the provocations suggested for Funnels, tubes and scoops

Literacy	Lit 1 speak	Lit 2 listen	Lit 3 group	Lit 4 drama	Lit 5 word	Lit 6 spell	Lit 7 text1	Lit 8 text2	Lit 9 text3	Lit10 text4	Lit11 sentence	Lit12 presentation
	1.1	2.1	3.1	4.1	5.1	6.1	7.1	8.1	9.1	10.1	11.1	12.1
	1.2	2.2	3.2	4.2	5.2	6.2	7.2	8.2	9.2	10.2	11.2	12.2

Numeracy	Num 1 U&A	Num 2 count	Num 3 number	Num 4 calculate	Num 5 shape	Num 6 measure	Num 7 data
	1.1	2.1	3.1	4.1	5.1	6.1	7.1
	1.2	2.2	3.2	4.2	5.2	6.2	7.2

Science	SC1 Enquiry			SC2 Life processes					SC3 Materials		SC4 Phys processes		
	Sc1.1	Sc1.2	Sc1.3	Sc2.1	Sc2.2	Sc2.3	Sc2.4	Sc2.5	Sc3.1	Sc3.2	Sc4.1	Sc4.2	Sc4.3
	1.1a	1.2a	1.3a	2.1a	2.2a	2.3a	2.4a	2.5a	3.1a	3.2a	4.1a	4.2a	4.3a
	1.1b	1.2b	1.3b	2.1b	2.2b	2.3b	2.4b	2.5b	3.1b	3.2b	4.1b	4.2b	4.3b
	1.1c	1.2c	1.3c	2.1c	2.2c	2.3c		2.5c	3.1c		4.1c	4.2c	4.3c
	1.1d				2.2d				3.1d				4.3d
					2.2e								
					2.2f								
					2.2g								

ICT	ICT 1 finding out		ICT 2 ideas	ICT 3 reviewing	ICT 4 breadth
	1.1a	1.2a	2a	3a	4a
	1.1b	1.2b	2b	3b	4b
	1.1c	1.2c	2c	3c	4c
		1.2d			

Full version of KS1 PoS on pages 69-74
Photopcopiable version on page 8

D&T	D&T 1 developing	D&T 2 tool use	D&T 3 evaluating	D&T 4 materials	D&T 5 breadth
	1a	2a	3a	4a	5a
	1b	2b	3b	4b	5b
	1c	2c			5c
	1d	2d			
	1e	2e			

History	H1 chronology	H2 events, people	H3 interpret	H4 enquire	H5 org & comm	H6 breadth
	1a	2a	3a	4a	5a	6a
	1b	2b		4b		6b
						6c
						6d

Geography	G1.1 & G1.2 enquiry		G2 places	G3 processes	G4 environment	G5 breadth
	1.1a	1.2a	2a	3a	4a	5a
	1.1b	1.2b	2b	3b	4b	5b
	1.1c	1.2c	2c			5c
	1.1d	1.2d	2d			5d
			2e			

Music	M1 performing	M2 composing	M3 appraising	M4 listening	M5 breadth
	1a	2a	3a	4a	5a
	1b	2b	3b	4b	5b
	1c			4c	5c
					5d

PHSE & C	PSHEC1 conf & resp	PSHEC2 citizenship	PSHEC3 health	PSHEC4 relationships
	1a	2a	3a	4a
	1b	2b	3b	4b
	1c	2c	3c	4c
	1d	2d	3d	4d
	1e	2e	3e	4e
		2f	3f	
		2g	3g	
		2h		

Art & Design	A&D1 ideas	A&D2 making	A&D3 evaluating	A&D4 materials	A&D5 breadth
	1a	2a	3a	4a	5a
	1b	2b	3b	4b	5b
		2c		4c	5c
					5d

PE	PE1 devel skills	PE2 apply skills	PE3 evaluate	PE4 fitness	PE5 breadth
	1a	2a	3a	4a	5a dance
	1b	2b	3b	4b	5b games
		2c	3c		5c gym

Photo copyright ASCO

Critical skills	Thinking Skills
problem solving	observing
decision making	classifying
critical thinking	prediction
creative thinking	making inferences
communication	problem solving
organisation	drawing conclusions
management	
leadership	

Sieves, jugs and containers

Sieves, jugs, containers

Previous experience in the Foundation Stage

These tools are also familiar in most Foundation Stage settings. Children will have used them:

* free play indoors and out of doors;
* in cooking activities for sieving lumps from flour or icing sugar;
* for straining pasta, vegetables and other foods cooked in water;
* with gloop, flour, seeds, dried pulses, foam and other malleable materials;
* in sand trays and builders' trays;
* for sieving small objects out of sand or water;
* in the garden to sieve and sort soil, compost or other natural materials;
* in domestic role play, cooking and making other food in role.

Pause for thought

In the early stages of working with these materials it is crucial to continue to observe the children. Only by doing this can you set developmentally appropriate challenges and provocations. The ideas listed here are offered as suggestions; the most exciting challenges will arise from children's own interests and motivations, which will only become apparent as you spend time with them, watching and joining them in their play. As you do this, you will be moving between the three interconnecting roles of observer, co-player, extender described below, and will be able to decide what you need to do next to take the learning forward.

The responsive adult (see page 5)

In three interconnecting roles, the responsive adult will be:

* observing
* listening
* interpreting

observer

* **modelling**
* **playing alongside**
* **offering suggestions**
* **responding sensitively**
* **initiating with care!**

co-player

* discussing ideas
* sharing thinking
* modelling new skills
* asking open questions
* being an informed extender
* instigating ideas & thoughts
* supporting children as they make links in learning
* making possibilities evident
* introducing new ideas and resources
* offering challenges and provocations

extender

Offering challenges and provocations - some ideas:

Small versions of sieves, whisks, containers, bowls, colanders etc can be found in cook shops, toyshops, bargain shops and DIY stores. Collect as many different sorts and sizes as you can, using them will help with motor skills in writing and reading.

? Use the sieves to explore sand, sawdust, gravel and soil. How do sieves work? What do they do?

? Add some grains of rice to dry sand. How can you use the sieves and colanders to get the rice grains out of the sand? Which one works best?

? Hold up a sieve or colander full of sand and watch carefully how the sand falls through the holes. What do you see? Why do you think it happens.

? Fill a jug with sand and pour it slowly into a sieve. Can your friend take a photo of what happens? Make a label for the photo and put it where other children can see it.

? Mix some dry sand and some sequins. Now add water till the sand is completely under water. What happens to the sequins? Can you catch them? What could you use?

? Mix some small toys in the dry sand. What is the best way to get them out again without touching the sand?

? Use a sieve or colander to fill a big bowl with sand. What happens? Is it the best tool to use? What would be a better tool?

? Mix some rice, sand, lentils and dried peas. Now try to sort them out again using the sieves and colanders. Is this easy? How can you do it?

? Find a big piece of paper and a colander or sieve. Now hold the colander or sieve over the paper and pour some sand through it. watch what the sand does as it falls on the paper. Take photos of the way sand falls through colanders and sieves with different sized holes or patterns. Try pouring slowly and very fast and watch what happens.

Carrying on in Key Stage 1

Providing c   exploration

Ros Bayley, Lynn Broadbent, Sally Featherstone

Published 2008 by A&C Black Publishers Limited
38 Soho Square, London W1D 3HB
www.acblack.com

First published 2007 by Featherstone Education Limited

ISBN 978-1-9060-2913-5

Text © Ros Bayley, Lyn Broadbent, Sally Featherstone 2008
Illustrations © Kerry Ingham 2008
Photographs © Lynn Broadbent, Ros Bayley,
Sally Featherstone, Sarah Featherstone 2008

A CIP record for this publication is available from the British Library.

Printed in Malta by Gutenberg Press Limited

This book is produced using paper that is made from wood grown in
managed, sustainable forests. It is natural, renewable and recyclable.
The logging and manufacturing processes conform to the environmental
regulations of the country of origin.

To see our full range of titles
visit **www.acblack.com**

Ready for more?

- Get some soil or compost. Mix it with water in a bowl or bucket till it is very wet. Now use the sieves to strain the watery mixture. What do you catch? What stays in the water? Why do some of the bits stay in the water? How could you get them out?

- Line a colander or sieve with paper towels and try this with a watery mixture of sand or compost. What happens?

- Does a colander or sieve work if you turn it upside down? What do you find out when you try? Why do you think this happens?

- Get some flour or icing sugar and tip it into a sieve. Shake the sieve. What happens? What is left in the sieve. Why do chefs sieve flour and icing sugar? Try shaking icing sugar or flour onto black paper. Can you make patterns?

- Roll out some dough or plasticene. Press a colander or sieve into the surface and look at what happens. Look inside the sieve and at the dough.

- Look at the pictures of a sieves on this page. Maybe you could borrow a garden sieve from someone who likes gardening. What is this sieve used for? How is it different from a kitchen sieve? Try it with some soil or compost.

- Pour water <u>slowly</u> through a small sieve or colander onto a thin layer of dry sand. What happens? Look at the patterns.

Materials, equipment suppliers, websites, books and other references

Suppliers of plastic containers, sieves and other sand toys:
ASCO www.ascoeducational.co.uk for general sand equipment.
TTS Group www.tts-group.co.uk for sieves and funnels and builder's trays.
You can also get builder's tray (cement mixing trays) from DIY superstores such as B&Q, Wilkinsons or Homebase. Garden sieves are cheap and durable. Get some cat litter trays or square washing up bowls from a Bargain Shop for space saving sand play.

Buy some big plastic plant saucers, windowsill plant trays or shallow planters from a garden centre for individual play on tables.

For useful images of sand play and equipment, try Google Images. Just enter the name or type of the tool or activity you want to see ('sieve' 'colander' 'sifter' 'strainer' etc) for hundreds of different sorts.

Send for some cookware catalogues such as Lakeland Plastics www.lakeland.co.uk

Google 'cooking equipment' for lots of sites.

Buy lentils, dried peas and beans and dry pasta in bulk from supermarkets or Asian/Italian wholesalers. You could ask your local shopkeepers (and the parents) for 'past the sell by date' pasta and pulses to make this activity more eco-friendly.

Some suitable books for younger readers include:
The Riddle of the Stolen Sand (a junior detective story); George Edward Stanley; Aladdin
The Sand Tray (Thinkers); Don Rowe; A&C Black
Sand and Soil (Rocks, Minerals, and Resources); Beth Gurney; Crabtree Publishing
Sand on the Move (First Books--Earth & Sky Science); Roy Gallant; Franklin Watts
Dazzling Diggers; Tody Mitton; Kingfisher Books
Diggers and Cranes; Jim Pipe; Franklin Watts.

Curriculum coverage grid overleaf

Potential NC KS1 Curriculum Coverage through the provocations suggested for Sieves, jugs and containers

Photo copyright ASCO

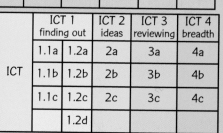

Photo copyright ASCO

Full version of KS1 PoS on pages 69-74
Photopcopiable version on page 8

Literacy

	Lit 1 speak	Lit 2 listen	Lit 3 group	Lit 4 drama	Lit 5 word	Lit 6 spell	Lit 7 text1	Lit 8 text2	Lit 9 text3	Lit10 text4	Lit11 sentence	Lit12 presentation
Literacy	1.1	2.1	3.1	4.1	5.1	6.1	7.1	8.1	9.1	10.1	11.1	12.1
	1.2	2.2	3.2	4.2	5.2	6.2	7.2	8.2	9.2	10.2	11.2	12.2

Numeracy

	Num 1 U&A	Num 2 count	Num 3 number	Num 4 calculate	Num 5 shape	Num 6 measure	Num 7 data
Numeracy	1.1	2.1	3.1	4.1	5.1	6.1	7.1
	1.2	2.2	3.2	4.2	5.2	6.2	7.2

Science

	SC1 Enquiry			SC2 Life processes					SC3 Materials		SC4 Phys processes		
	Sc1.1	Sc1.2	Sc1.3	Sc2.1	Sc2.2	Sc2.3	Sc2.4	Sc2.5	Sc3.1	Sc3.2	Sc4.1	Sc4.2	Sc4.3
Science	1.1a	1.2a	1.3a	2.1a	2.2a	2.3a	2.4a	2.5a	3.1a	3.2a	4.1a	4.2a	4.3a
	1.1b	1.2b	1.3b	2.1b	2.2b	2.3b	2.4b	2.5b	3.1b	3.2b	4.1b	4.2b	4.3b
	1.1c	1.2c	1.3c	2.1c	2.2c	2.3c		2.5c	3.1c		4.1c	4.2c	4.3c
	1.1d				2.2d				3.1d				4.3d
					2.2e								
					2.2f								
					2.2g								

ICT

	ICT 1 finding out	ICT 2 ideas	ICT 3 reviewing	ICT 4 breadth
ICT	1.1a	1.2a	2a	3a	4a
	1.1b	1.2b	2b	3b	4b
	1.1c	1.2c	2c	3c	4c
		1.2d			

History

	H1 chronology	H2 events, people	H3 interpret	H4 enquire	H5 org & comm	H6 breadth
History	1a	2a	3a	4a	5a	6a
	1b	2b		4b		6b
						6c
						6d

Geography

	G1.1 & G1.2 enquiry		G2 places	G3 processes	G4 environment	G5 breadth
Geography	1.1a	1.2a	2a	3a	4a	5a
	1.1b	1.2b	2b	3b	4b	5b
	1.1c	1.2c	2c			5c
	1.1d	1.2d	2d			5d
			2e			

D&T

	D&T 1 developing	D&T 2 tool use	D&T 3 evaluating	D&T 4 materials	D&T 5 breadth
D&T	1a	2a	3a	4a	5a
	1b	2b	3b	4b	5b
	1c	2c			5c
	1d	2d			
	1e	2e			

Music

	M1 performing	M2 composing	M3 appraising	M4 listening	M5 breadth
Music	1a	2a	3a	4a	5a
	1b	2b	3b	4b	5b
	1c			4c	5c
					5d

PHSE & C

	PSHEC1 conf & resp	PSHEC2 citizenship	PSHEC3 health	PSHEC4 relationships
PHSE & C	1a	2a	3a	4a
	1b	2b	3b	4b
	1c	2c	3c	4c
	1d	2d	3d	4d
	1e	2e	3e	4e
		2f	3f	
		2g	3g	
		2h		

Art & Design

	A&D1 ideas	A&D2 making	A&D3 evaluating	A&D4 materials	A&D5 breadth
Art & Design	1a	2a	3a	4a	5a
	1b	2b	3b	4b	5b
		2c		4c	5c
					5d

PE

	PE1 devel skills	PE2 apply skills	PE3 evaluate	PE4 fitness	PE5 breadth
PE	1a	2a	3a	4a	5a dance
	1b	2b	3b	4b	5b games
		2c	3c		5c gym

Critical skills / Thinking Skills

Critical skills	Thinking Skills
problem solving	observing
decision making	classifying
critical thinking	prediction
creative thinking	making inferences
communication	problem solving
organisation	drawing conclusions
management	
leadership	

Small world

Small world

Previous experience in the Foundation Stage

By the time children leave the Foundation Stage they should have had extensive experience of constructing small worlds:

* in free play indoors and out of doors;
* in role play situations;
* in play with builders' trays and story boxes;
* to explore ways of making steady structures;
* when playing with train sets and play mats;
* in sand and water play;
* when playing with clay, dough, malleable materials.

They will also have had experience of:

* developing narratives and constructing scenarios;
* using fine motor skills to place objects.

Pause for thought

In the early stages of working with these materials it is crucial to continue to observe the children. Only by doing this can you set developmentally appropriate challenges and provocations. The ideas listed here are offered as suggestions; the most exciting challenges will arise from children's own interests and motivations, which will only become apparent as you spend time with them, watching and joining them in their play. As you do this, you will be moving between the three interconnecting roles of observer, co-player, extender described below, and will be able to decide what you need to do next to take the learning forward.

The responsive adult (see page 5)

In three interconnecting roles, the responsive adult will be:

* observing
* listening
* interpreting

observer

* **modelling**
* **playing alongside**
* **offering suggestions**
* **responding sensitively**
* **initiating with care!**

co-player

* discussing ideas
* sharing thinking
* modelling new skills
* asking open questions
* being an informed extender
* instigating ideas & thoughts
* supporting children as they make links in learning
* making possibilities evident
* introducing new ideas and resources
* offering challenges and provocations

extender

Offering challenges and provocations - some ideas:

Children may need practice in accepting and carrying out challenges presented by adults, when they have been used to free play in sand. You may need to introduce this gradually and sit with the children as they work to encourage them to stay on task!

? Can you make a plan or a list of the materials you need to make a jungle in the sand? Collect the things you need and build the jungle according to your plan.

? Can you build a space station for astronauts? a farm for some animals? a desert island, a town or a village?

? Look on Google Images 'jungle' or 'rainforest' and use the pictures to help you build a scene.

? Write a jungle story and then make some scenes to photograph for the illustrations.

? Use books to help you find out about animals, birds and plants that live in rainforests and jungles. Use the information to help you with your project.

? Read a jungle story and make some scenes of different parts of the story. Photograph your scenes. Add some play people and make a jungle diary for the explorers.

? Watch 'Jungle Book', 'Finding Nemo', 'Charlotte's Web' or another film, and make a replica of your favourite scene from the film, complete with animals and people.

? When you are at home or outside, look for objects that you could use for your small world scenes - leaves, twigs, stones, bark, seeds, nuts and acorns. Use these to make your own stories by adding small people or animals.

? Use small boxes or cartons to make buildings for your scenes, or find some small blocks of wood that you can make into buildings by drawing windows and doors on the surfaces.

? Make a small world version of your house or your bedroom with furniture, people and other objects.

Ready for more?

- Read 'Where the Forest Meets the Sea'. Collect some twigs, shells, stones, branches to make replicas of some of the scenes in the story.

- Visit a garden centre and find pot plants that grow in jungles and rain-forests. Buy some small ones to add to your scenes. Photograph your jungles.

- Mix some sand with compost and plant some seeds to make our jungle even more realistic. Try grass seed, mustard and cress, or rocket. Remember to keep the seeds moist by spraying them with a hand sprayer.

- Now use the skills you have as jungle designers to make other sorts of land-scapes - mountains, islands, forests, arctic lands, rivers and streams. Use books and the internet to find information. Photograph your creations and make an exhibition or a book.

- Make some background scenery for your small worlds. Use card from cartons or boxes and paint mountains, cities, other planets, castles or other places to make the world more realistic. Take some photos of your creations for a story book or class collection, which you could use as an ideas book for stories and poems.

- Try to get a plastic aquarium and make an underground world with tunnels and caves that you can see though the sides.

Materials, equipment suppliers, websites, books and other references

Small world animals and people are available from all **educational suppliers**. There is a huge variety and range of types in suppliers catalogues and on their websites. Many suppliers have 'own brand' versions of small world sets, which are often cheaper, but may not be as realistic or durable. As with all educational equipment, you will get what you pay for - buy the best you can afford. For instance:

ASCO www.ascoeducational.co.uk have Counting Kids (a box of 100 small world children), collections of insects, frogs etc, a collection of woodland animals.

Early Learning Centre www.elc.co.uk have baby wild animals, dinosaur models of various sizes and farm animals.

Britains www.toyandmodel.com/britains have a huge range of farm animals in families, farm vehicles, tractors and farm people. They also make fences, hay bales, animal shelters etc.

Playmobil www.playmobil.com have themed characters and a great range of fantasy settings, vehicles and accessories which are firm favourites of all children.

Consortium groups can often offer class or group Lego and other sets with huge numbers of pieces. Add some more specialised pieces, wheels, people, trees etc. from local suppliers or the Lego website www.lego.com for variety and inspiration.

Familiar stories and picture books will give endless ideas for small world activities in sand, with simple additions of natural materials.

Some more books for young readers who may need a bit of new inspiration:

Where the Forest Meets the Sea; Jeannie Baker; Walker Books
The Sand Horse; Ann Turnbull; Andersen Press
Sand Sister; Amanda White; Barefoot Books
The Great Kapok Tree; Lynne Cherry; Harcourt
A Walk in the Rainforest; Kristin Joy Pratt; Dawn Publications
Amazon River Rescue; Amanda Lumry; Eaglemont Press
The Case of the Dinosaur in the Desert; Pauline Hutchens-Wilson; Moody Publishers (A New Sugar Street Gang Story).

Curriculum coverage grid overleaf

Potential NC KS1 Curriculum Coverage through the provocations suggested for small world scenes

Full version of KS1 PoS on pages 69-74
Photocopiable version on page 8

Literacy	Lit 1 speak	Lit 2 listen	Lit 3 group	Lit 4 drama	Lit 5 word	Lit 6 spell	Lit 7 text1	Lit 8 text2	Lit 9 text3	Lit10 text4	Lit11 sentence	Lit12 presentation
	1.1	2.1	3.1	4.1	5.1	6.1	7.1	8.1	9.1	10.1	11.1	12.1
	1.2	2.2	3.2	4.2	5.2	6.2	7.2	8.2	9.2	10.2	11.2	12.2

Numeracy	Num 1 U&A	Num 2 count	Num 3 number	Num 4 calculate	Num 5 shape	Num 6 measure	Num 7 data
	1.1	2.1	3.1	4.1	5.1	6.1	7.1
	1.2	2.2	3.2	4.2	5.2	6.2	7.2

Science	SC1 Enquiry			SC2 Life processes					SC3 Materials		SC4 Phys processes		
	Sc1.1	Sc1.2	Sc1.3	Sc2.1	Sc2.2	Sc2.3	Sc2.4	Sc2.5	Sc3.1	Sc3.2	Sc4.1	Sc4.2	Sc4.3
	1.1a	1.2a	1.3a	2.1a	2.2a	2.3a	2.4a	2.5a	3.1a	3.2a	4.1a	4.2a	4.3a
	1.1b	1.2b	1.3b	2.1b	2.2b	2.3b	2.4b	2.5b	3.1b	3.2b	4.1b	4.2b	4.3b
	1.1c	1.2c	1.3c	2.1c	2.2c	2.3c		2.5c	3.1c		4.1c	4.2c	4.3c
	1.1d				2.2d				3.1d				4.3d
					2.2e								
					2.2f								
					2.2g								

ICT	ICT 1 finding out		ICT 2 ideas	ICT 3 reviewing	ICT 4 breadth
	1.1a	1.2a	2a	3a	4a
	1.1b	1.2b	2b	3b	4b
	1.1c	1.2c	2c	3c	4c
		1.2d			

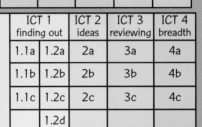

D&T	D&T 1 developing	D&T 2 tool use	D&T 3 evaluating	D&T 4 materials	D&T 5 breadth
	1a	2a	3a	4a	5a
	1b	2b	3b	4b	5b
	1c	2c			5c
	1d	2d			
	1e	2e			

History	H1 chronology	H2 events, people	H3 interpret	H4 enquire	H5 org & comm	H6 breadth
	1a	2a	3a	4a	5a	6a
	1b	2b		4b		6b
						6c
						6d

Geography	G1.1 & G1.2 enquiry		G2 places	G3 processes	G4 environment	G5 breadth
	1.1a	1.2a	2a	3a	4a	5a
	1.1b	1.2b	2b	3b	4b	5b
	1.1c	1.2c	2c			5c
	1.1d	1.2d	2d			5d
			2e			

Music	M1 performing	M2 composing	M3 appraising	M4 listening	M5 breadth
	1a	2a	3a	4a	5a
	1b	2b	3b	4b	5b
	1c			4c	5c
					5d

PHSE & C	PSHEC1 conf & resp	PSHEC2 citizenship	PSHEC3 health	PSHEC4 relationships
	1a	2a	3a	4a
	1b	2b	3b	4b
	1c	2c	3c	4c
	1d	2d	3d	4d
	1e	2e	3e	4e
		2f	3f	
		2g	3g	
		2h		

Art & Design	A&D1 ideas	A&D2 making	A&D3 evaluating	A&D4 materials	A&D5 breadth
	1a	2a	3a	4a	5a
	1b	2b	3b	4b	5b
		2c		4c	5c
					5d

PE	PE1 devel skills	PE2 apply skills	PE3 evaluate	PE4 fitness	PE5 breadth
	1a	2a	3a	4a	5a dance
	1b	2b	3b	4b	5b games
		2c	3c		5c gym

Critical skills	Thinking Skills
problem solving	observing
decision making	classifying
critical thinking	prediction
creative thinking	making inferences
communication	problem solving
organisation	drawing conclusions
management	
leadership	

Gardens

Gardens

Previous experience in the Foundation Stage

Making gardens is a classic childhood activity, whether they are for superheroes or doll's tea-parties. Children may have had experience of making gardens:

* in free play indoors and out of doors;
* combined with small world to make story settings;
* combined with fantasy worlds (dinosaurs, princes and princesses, wizards and dragons, superheroes etc);
* combined with malleable materials to make habitats for toys, creatures, vehicles;
* to explore natural materials such as petals, leaves, seeds, stones, bark and twigs;
* to explore free recall of stories they have heard and experiences they have had in real life;
* to explore relationships and feelings in small world play.

Pause for thought

In the early stages of working with these materials it is crucial to continue to observe the children. Only by doing this can you set developmentally appropriate challenges and provocations. The ideas listed here are offered as suggestions; the most exciting challenges will arise from children's own interests and motivations, which will only become apparent as you spend time with them, watching and joining them in their play. As you do this, you will be moving between the three interconnecting roles of observer, co-player, extender described below, and will be able to decide what you need to do next to take the learning forward.

The responsive adult (see page 5)

In three interconnecting roles, the responsive adult will be:

* observing
* listening
* interpreting

observer

* **modelling**
* **playing alongside**
* **offering suggestions**
* **responding sensitively**
* **initiating with care!**

co-player

* discussing ideas
* sharing thinking
* modelling new skills
* asking open questions
* being an informed extender
* instigating ideas & thoughts
* supporting children as they make links in learning
* making possibilities evident
* introducing new ideas and resources
* offering challenges and provocations

extender

Offering challenges and provocations - some ideas:

Making gardens is a creative and therapeutic activity, which most children love. In the Foundation Stage this will probably have been a free choice, child-initiated activity, and you may have to sit with the children and help them to keep on task if you want to challenge their creativity in particular ways. Some children may never have made a miniature garden, so be patient and give plenty of scope for individual responses! Builders' trays are ideal, but paper or plastic plates are good for individuals.

? Can you make a garden with stones, pebbles and sand? Now go outside and collect some other things to make your garden more interesting. You can use anything you find, just make sure it will fit.

? Choose three small world animals or people and make a garden for them.

? Can you make a garden for some dinosaurs? They need plenty of things to eat.

? Find some foil and make a riverside or seaside garden, or a pond in a garden. Add some other objects and people to make it more realistic.

? Make a playground for children. Design it first on paper, then collect the things you need.

? Make a garden with just sand and leaves of different sorts, sizes and shapes. Use them to make paths and flower beds as well.

? Make a garden for a story character. Take some photos and make a book to show with the story book.

? Look carefully at a real life garden (your own at home or one you like). Take some photos if you can. Now recreate your garden in the sand tray, making it as realistic as you can. Use anything that makes the garden look interesting, foil, small furniture, people, pets, animals and birds. You could draw these or cut them from gardening magazines or catalogues. Stick them on card and find a way to make them stand up.

Ready for more?

- What sort of garden would a superhero like? Design and make it for them. Add some character pictures that you have drawn or cut from magazines.

- Can you make a garden for a person who likes sitting and reading out of doors? You will need to think about the weather! Draw your ideas, then make a model of your garden.

- Design and make a garden with no plants. Think about what else can go in a garden to make it look interesting and welcoming.

- Get some grass seed and sprinkle it on damp sand or mud. Don't forget to water it with a small sprayer while it grows into a lawn.

- Collect some twigs, branches and leaves and make a garden for hedgehogs, frogs, toads and lizards. Make some animals from dough, clay or plasticene to live in your garden.

- Make a garden for your favourite story character (or a favourite member of your family). Fill it with the things they like.

- Try growing some real plants in sand. You could try hyacinth, daffodil or tulip bulbs or beans and peas. If you put the sand in a clear plastic bottle (the bottom of a water bottle works well) you will be able to see the roots growing. Remember to water them, but don't let them get too wet. Take a series of photos or drawings of the growth of your plants.

Materials, equipment suppliers, websites, books and other references

Making gardens is a therapeutic and creative activity. The children can quickly collect the natural materials they need from home or school, and you can add an occasional bargain bunch of flowers or some leaves or twigs you have collected. You can use plates, old trays, plant saucers, shallow plastic boxes, packaging trays, or other shallow, waterproof containers as bases. This way, several children can work at the same time, and inspire each other. If they need some ideas, offer some gardening books or go on a local walk to look at gardens in the neighbourhood.

You could put 'flower' 'garden' 'garden design' 'flowerbed' 'parterre' in Google Images or look at some websites of garden designers:

www.gardenplans.com has hundreds of garden plans to look at and download
www.applegategardens.co.uk look at 'garden design' for lots of lovely ideas for different sorts of gardens.
www.bbc.co.uk/gardening/design has lots of designs by TV garden designers.
www.gardendesigner.com where you can view and download free designs.
www.rhs.org.uk/advice/design/design2 for pictures of Chelsea.
www.uktv.co.uk/index.cfm/uktv/Gardens for children's garden plans.
www.bbc.co.uk/gardening/gardening_with_children lots of ideas, projects, things to do.
www.allotments-uk.com/links/gardening for kids
www.gardenorganic.org.uk/schools_organic_network/index a good site with ideas, curriculum links, activities etc, which might help with designing a garden.
www.ltl.org.uk Learning Through Landscapes - is an inspiring charitable organisation which will help with information on all aspects of the outdoors. Look at some of the projects they have supported.

Some **book** titles:
How Does your Garden Grow? Clare Matthews; Hamlyn
Roots, Shoots, Buckets and Boots; Sharon Lovejoy; Workman Publishing
Gardening with Children; Kim Wilde; Harper Collins.

Curriculum coverage grid overleaf

Potential NC KS1 Curriculum Coverage through the provocations suggested for gardens

Full version of KS1 PoS on pages 69-74
Photopcopiable version on page 8

Literacy

	Lit 1 speak	Lit 2 listen	Lit 3 group	Lit 4 drama	Lit 5 word	Lit 6 spell	Lit 7 text1	Lit 8 text2	Lit 9 text3	Lit10 text4	Lit11 sentence	Lit12 presentation
Literacy	1.1	2.1	3.1	4.1	5.1	6.1	7.1	8.1	9.1	10.1	11.1	12.1
	1.2	2.2	3.2	4.2	5.2	6.2	7.2	8.2	9.2	10.2	11.2	12.2

Numeracy

	Num 1 U&A	Num 2 count	Num 3 number	Num 4 calculate	Num 5 shape	Num 6 measure	Num 7 data
Numeracy	1.1	2.1	3.1	4.1	5.1	6.1	7.1
	1.2	2.2	3.2	4.2	5.2	6.2	7.2

Science

	SC1 Enquiry			SC2 Life processes					SC3 Materials		SC4 Phys processes		
	Sc1.1	Sc1.2	Sc1.3	Sc2.1	Sc2.2	Sc2.3	Sc2.4	Sc2.5	Sc3.1	Sc3.2	Sc4.1	Sc4.2	Sc4.3
Science	1.1a	1.2a	1.3a	2.1a	2.2a	2.3a	2.4a	2.5a	3.1a	3.2a	4.1a	4.2a	4.3a
	1.1b	1.2b	1.3b	2.1b	2.2b	2.3b	2.4b	2.5b	3.1b	3.2b	4.1b	4.2b	4.3b
	1.1c	1.2c	1.3c	2.1c	2.2c	2.3c		2.5c	3.1c		4.1c	4.2c	4.3c
	1.1d				2.2d				3.1d				4.3d
					2.2e								
					2.2f								
					2.2g								

ICT

	ICT 1 finding out		ICT 2 ideas	ICT 3 reviewing	ICT 4 breadth
	1.1a	1.2a	2a	3a	4a
ICT	1.1b	1.2b	2b	3b	4b
	1.1c	1.2c	2c	3c	4c
		1.2d			

D&T

	D&T 1 developing	D&T 2 tool use	D&T 3 evaluating	D&T 4 materials	D&T 5 breadth
	1a	2a	3a	4a	5a
D&T	1b	2b	3b	4b	5b
	1c	2c			5c
	1d	2d			
	1e	2e			

History

	H1 chronology	H2 events, people	H3 interpret	H4 enquire	H5 org & comm	H6 breadth
	1a	2a	3a	4a	5a	6a
History	1b	2b		4b		6b
						6c
						6d

Geography

	G1.1 & G1.2 enquiry		G2 places	G3 processes	G4 environment	G5 breadth
	1.1a	1.2a	2a	3a	4a	5a
Geography	1.1b	1.2b	2b	3b	4b	5b
	1.1c	1.2c	2c			5c
	1.1d	1.2d	2d			5d
			2e			

Music

	M1 performing	M2 composing	M3 appraising	M4 listening	M5 breadth
	1a	2a	3a	4a	5a
Music	1b	2b	3b	4b	5b
	1c			4c	5c
					5d

PHSE & C

	PSHEC1 conf & resp	PSHEC2 citizenship	PSHEC3 health	PSHEC4 relationships
	1a	2a	3a	4a
	1b	2b	3b	4b
PHSE & C	1c	2c	3c	4c
	1d	2d	3d	4d
	1e	2e	3e	4e
		2f	3f	
		2g	3g	
		2h		

Art & Design

	A&D1 ideas	A&D2 making	A&D3 evaluating	A&D4 materials	A&D5 breadth
	1a	2a	3a	4a	5a
Art & Design	1b	2b	3b	4b	5b
		2c		4c	5c
					5d

PE

	PE1 devel skills	PE2 apply skills	PE3 evaluate	PE4 fitness	PE5 breadth
	1a	2a	3a	4a	5a dance
PE	1b	2b	3b	4b	5b games
		2c	3c		5c gym

Critical skills	Thinking Skills
problem solving	observing
decision making	classifying
critical thinking	prediction
creative thinking	making inferences
communication	problem solving
organisation	drawing conclusions
management	
leadership	

Delta sand and moulding

Delta Sand and moulding

Previous experience in the Foundation Stage

Moulding sand is a popular activity in the Foundation Stage. Delta Sand is a commercial version of sand, which is more permanent and can be sculpted. Children would have used sculpting and moulding techniques in sand:

* in free play with sand and mud indoors and out of doors;
* combined with small world people and other figures to make habitats, roadways, bridges and tunnels;
* with sand and malleable materials to make models and structures;
* to explore shape, texture and form;
* to count and order;
* to explore pattern and repeating patterns.

Pause for thought

In the early stages of working with these materials it is crucial to continue to observe the children. Only by doing this can you set developmentally appropriate challenges and provocations. The ideas listed here are offered as suggestions; the most exciting challenges will arise from children's own interests and motivations, which will only become apparent as you spend time with them, watching and joining them in their play. As you do this, you will be moving between the three interconnecting roles of observer, co-player, extender described below, and will be able to decide what you need to do next to take the learning forward.

The responsive adult (see page 5)

In three interconnecting roles, the responsive adult will be:

observer

* observing
* listening
* interpreting

co-player

* **modelling**
* **playing alongside**
* **offering suggestions**
* **responding sensitively**
* **initiating with care!**

extender

* discussing ideas
* sharing thinking
* modelling new skills
* asking open questions
* being an informed extender
* instigating ideas & thoughts
* supporting children as they make links in learning
* making possibilities evident
* introducing new ideas and resources
* offering challenges and provocations

Offering challenges and provocations - some ideas:

Provide a range of moulds for sand and Delta Sand, including moulds made for sand and jelly - collect small metal and plastic containers such as flower pots, yogurt pots, plastic caps of different sizes, little cups and bowls, shells, trays from chocolate boxes, cakes and tarts, plastic inserts from packaging, egg cartons.

? Explore all the different moulds and packaging and choose some favourites to make patterns and designs.

? Make a repeating pattern of two or three different sand moulds. See if your friend can continue the pattern.

? Use moulds with some coloured sand to make patterns and designs like chocolates and sweets. Decorate them with sequins or beads.

? Use some bigger moulds to make castles or blocks and decorate these with beads, sequins, shells and pebbles.

? Use a shallow flat tray to make a mould that you can write on with a sharp stick or a pencil. Now you can draw pictures, make patterns or write messages to your friends. A plant spray filled with water will keep the sand damp, so your marks don't disappear.

? Make some towers or other moulds with the sand and then make walls to link them into a castle or city wall.

? Look around at home and at school, for more ordinary and unusual objects that can be used as moulds with sand. Take some photos of the moulds and the patterns they make. You could make a catalogue for other children to use, with photos of the mould and what the sand looks like after moulding.

? Have a sandcastle competition with your friends. In pairs, take turns to make the best castle you can, take some photos of it and then let the next pair have a go. Get your teacher to look at the castles and the photos and judge the winner.

Ready for more?

- Look for jelly moulds in car boot sales and charity shops. Use these to make bigger models and castles, and decorate them with sequins, shells, stones, glass beads. You could also use these moulds to make castles of ice, cooked rice, clay or mud.
- Make a village or a whole city with small moulds. You could add white glue to the sand so the moulds don't dry out. Add gravel streets, people and vehicles to your city. Could you use the same method to make a fantasy scene with mountains, castles, bridges and houses?
- Get some Delta Sand and see what you can do with it. It's not as easy as it looks on the box! Take photos and make a book of tips for modelling with this 'sticky sand'.
- Look up 'sandcastle competition' on Google Images and see what you can find. Use the pictures as ideas for new ways of making sand look like stone. Have a new competition for making animals or landscapes with moulds and free work in the sand.
- Expand your collection of moulds and sand shapers by collecting foil dishes, cups, plastic bowls, shells, and other containers.
- Try making moulds with very wet sand and then freezing them overnight. What happens?

Materials, equipment suppliers, websites, books and other references

Use your ingenuity to find as many containers for moulding as you can. Packaging is a great source. Search for unusual sorts of sand moulds and jelly moulds to add - car boot sales, charity shops, bargain shops and cookware catalogues will often offer new ideas.

Add a range of small objects to decorate moulded sand - shells, sequins, beads, seeds, unusual items from pot pourri such as dried flowers and seed cases, buttons, badges, small world figures, cutlery etc.

Delta Sand, a mouldable sort of sand is available from www.deltasand.com where you can also see some finished projects. This sand is very different from plain sand and some children may become frustrated by it - give some time and support.

Another unusual sort of sand is Underwater Sculpting Sand which clings together for moulding underwater, but returns to its former state when you remove it from the water Amazon www.amazon.co.uk stock this product.

For images of sand sculptures, try Google Images, starting with 'sandcastle' 'sand sculpture' 'sand art' 'sand figure' 'beach art' 'beach sculpture'.

Some suitable books for younger readers include:
Art from Sand and Earth; Gillian Chapman; Hodder Wayland
Drawing in the Sand: Jerry Butler; Zino Press Children's Books: a book about African American artists.
Super Sand Castle Saturday (Mathstart); Stuart Murphy; Harper Collins
Sandcastles Made Simple; Lucinda Weirenga; Stewart, Tabori, Chang
The Sand Horse; Ann Turnbull; Andersen Press: a sand horse comes to life
Sand (Little Hands); Rachael Matthews; Chrysalis.

Curriculum coverage grid overleaf

Potential NC KS1 Curriculum Coverage through the provocations suggested for moulding

Full version of KS1 PoS on pages 69-74
Photopcopiable version on page 8

Literacy

	Lit 1 speak	Lit 2 listen	Lit 3 group	Lit 4 drama	Lit 5 word	Lit 6 spell	Lit 7 text1	Lit 8 text2	Lit 9 text3	Lit10 text4	Lit11 sentence	Lit12 presentation
	1.1	2.1	3.1	4.1	5.1	6.1	7.1	8.1	9.1	10.1	11.1	12.1
	1.2	2.2	3.2	4.2	5.2	6.2	7.2	8.2	9.2	10.2	11.2	12.2

Numeracy

	Num 1 U&A	Num 2 count	Num 3 number	Num 4 calculate	Num 5 shape	Num 6 measure	Num 7 data
	1.1	2.1	3.1	4.1	5.1	6.1	7.1
	1.2	2.2	3.2	4.2	5.2	6.2	7.2

Science

SC1 Enquiry			SC2 Life processes					SC3 Materials		SC4 Phys processes		
Sc1.1	Sc1.2	Sc1.3	Sc2.1	Sc2.2	Sc2.3	Sc2.4	Sc2.5	Sc3.1	Sc3.2	Sc4.1	Sc4.2	Sc4.3
1.1a	1.2a	1.3a	2.1a	2.2a	2.3a	2.4a	2.5a	3.1a	3.2a	4.1a	4.2a	4.3a
1.1b	1.2b	1.3b	2.1b	2.2b	2.3b	2.4b	2.5b	3.1b	3.2b	4.1b	4.2b	4.3b
1.1c	1.2c	1.3c	2.1c	2.2c	2.3c		2.5c	3.1c		4.1c	4.2c	4.3c
1.1d				2.2d				3.1d				4.3d
				2.2e								
				2.2f								
				2.2g								

ICT

	ICT 1 finding out		ICT 2 ideas	ICT 3 reviewing	ICT 4 breadth
	1.1a	1.2a	2a	3a	4a
	1.1b	1.2b	2b	3b	4b
	1.1c	1.2c	2c	3c	4c
		1.2d			

History

	H1 chronology	H2 events, people	H3 interpret	H4 enquire	H5 org & comm	H6 breadth
	1a	2a	3a	4a	5a	6a
	1b	2b		4b		6b
						6c
						6d

Geography

	G1.1 & G1.2 enquiry		G2 places	G3 processes	G4 environment	G5 breadth
	1.1a	1.2a	2a	3a	4a	5a
	1.1b	1.2b	2b	3b	4b	5b
	1.1c	1.2c	2c			5c
	1.1d	1.2d	2d			5d
			2e			

D&T

	D&T 1 developing	D&T 2 tool use	D&T 3 evaluating	D&T 4 materials	D&T 5 breadth
	1a	2a	3a	4a	5a
	1b	2b	3b	4b	5b
	1c	2c			5c
	1d	2d			
	1e	2e			

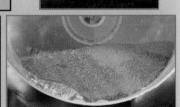

Music

	M1 performing	M2 composing	M3 appraising	M4 listening	M5 breadth
	1a	2a	3a	4a	5a
	1b	2b	3b	4b	5b
	1c			4c	5c
					5d

PHSE & C

	PSHEC1 conf & resp	PSHEC2 citizenship	PSHEC3 health	PSHEC4 relationships
	1a	2a	3a	4a
	1b	2b	3b	4b
	1c	2c	3c	4c
	1d	2d	3d	4d
	1e	2e	3e	4e
		2f	3f	
		2g	3g	
		2h		

Art & Design

	A&D1 ideas	A&D2 making	A&D3 evaluating	A&D4 materials	A&D5 breadth
	1a	2a	3a	4a	5a
	1b	2b	3b	4b	5b
		2c		4c	5c
					5d

PE

	PE1 devel skills	PE2 apply skills	PE3 evaluate	PE4 fitness	PE5 breadth
	1a	2a	3a	4a	5a dance
	1b	2b	3b	4b	5b games
		2c	3c		5c gym

Critical skills	Thinking Skills
problem solving	observing
decision making	classifying
critical thinking	prediction
creative thinking	making inferences
communication	problem solving
organisation	drawing conclusions
management	
leadership	

Teeny Tiny

Teeny tiny

Previous experience in the Foundation Stage

Children may have had experience of working with a variety of moulds and containers:

* making mud pies and sand castles;
* packing sand into containers of different sizes and shapes, and tipping it out;
* moulding wet sand with their hands;
* exploring spatial relationships on 3D;
* moving sand around to create hills, tunnels and smooth areas;
* pushing and poking things into sand - brushes, sticks, pencils, flags;
* making impressions in sand;
* adding water to sand and exploring what happens.

Pause for thought

In the early stages of working with these materials it is crucial to continue to observe the children. Only by doing this can you set developmentally appropriate challenges and provocations. The ideas listed here are offered as suggestions; the most exciting challenges will arise from children's own interests and motivations, which will only become apparent as you spend time with them, watching and joining them in their play. As you do this, you will be moving between the three interconnecting roles of observer, co-player, extender described below, and will be able to decide what you need to do next to take the learning forward.

The responsive adult (see page 5)

In three interconnecting roles, the responsive adult will be:

* observing
* listening
* interpreting

 observer

* **modelling**
* **playing alongside**
* **offering suggestions**
* **responding sensitively**
* **initiating with care!**

co-player

* discussing ideas
* sharing thinking
* modelling new skills
* asking open questions
* being an informed extender
* instigating ideas & thoughts
* supporting children as they make links in learning
* making possibilities evident
* introducing new ideas and resources
* offering challenges and provocations

extender

Offering challenges and provocations - some ideas:

Provide a range of small metal and plastic containers such as small flower pots, yogurt pots, plastic caps of different sizes, little cups and bowls, shells, little plastic bottles, plastic trays from chocolate boxes, cakes and tarts, egg cartons etc. You could also provide pictures of structures and buildings as inspiration for their constructions.

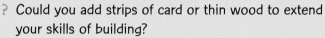

? Could you add strips of card or thin wood to extend your skills of building?

? Can you build a house, block of flats, church, railway station using sand and the pots and lids?

? Can you build a column of sand to support a small figure - like Nelson's Column?

? Can you make a home for a toy dinosaur or other jungle or wild animal?

? Can you build a tower with a series of moulds that decrease in size?

? Measure out a bowl or small bucket of sand. What is the highest structure you can build from this sand and the small moulding shapes? What is the longest structure you can make?

? Choose a small mould and see if you can build a structure using just this one mould. Can you make something from 20 mouldings? Or 30? or 100? You may need to draw the design first.

? Can you make a replica of the Coliseum, the Great Wall of China, The Acropolis?

? Look in the recycled materials for some containers that you could use as moulds. You could cut some plastic containers to make different shapes and sizes, or cut card and stick it together to make little box shapes.

? Try cutting some plastic containers or water bottles. Look around the classroom for containers that you could use for moulding bricks and shapes from sand.

Ready for more?

- Add tubes, boxes and card to your collection of moulds. Can you make a skyline or a whole city with these?
- Can you make a city of the future and add rockets and people?
- Collect lots of different moulds. Which ones work best? Why? Make a chart of what you discover.
- Make a plan or write a description for a structure or city. Challenge your friend to build it.
- Use the moulds to make some sleeping creatures - dinosaurs, dragons, monsters in the sand. They could be almost covered with the sand, like fossils or frozen in a deep freeze!
- Get some clay or mud and mix it with some sand. Use your moulds to make some bricks. Leave them to dry and then use them to make walls, buildings and other structures.
- Can you make a very, very small village with damp sand? Use cocktail sticks, small spoons, lolly sticks or twigs to help you with the details of doors, windows, gardens and fields. Find or make some tiny people and animals to live in your tiny village.
- Flatten out some damp sand and use a pencil or a stick to make mazes in the surface. Challenge a friend to find their way.

Materials, equipment suppliers, websites, books and other references

Some ideas for **resources and equipment**:

Educational suppliers have endless supplies that can help with these activities. Look for small scoops, bun tins and cases, sand moulds and small objects to make patterns and impressions in the surface.

Recycled materials also offer lots of opportunities to work on a small scale. These include:

the liners from boxes of chocolates

small foil cases from cakes and pies

plastic caps of all sorts and sizes - from toothpaste tubes to aerosol caps

ice cream spoons, straws, ice cream cups

packaging plastic that you can cut down to make interesting shapes

coins, shells and buttons.

Google images: 'miniature', 'miniature houses', 'doll's house', 'model great wall of china' which brings up lots of pictures or 'model acropolis' 'model city' 'wall' or 'tower' will give help with structures, and 'Nelson's column' will help with the column challenge

Try www.museumofminiatures.org for dolls houses.

www.essexminiatures.co.uk where you can click on individual models of Romans and Ancient Britons.

www.goodies-dollshouse-miniatures.co.uk has a new photo of a miniature every week.

Books and Publications:

Avoid Working on the Great Wall of China: Jacqueline Morley; Book House

The Great Wall; Elizabeth Mann; Miyaka Press

The Roman Colosseum; Elizabeth Mann; Miyaka Press

Skyscrapers and Bridges - Super Structures to design and build; Carol Johmann; Williamson

Structures, Materials and Art Activities; Barbara Taylor; Crabtree Publishing.

Curriculum coverage grid overleaf

Potential NC KS1 Curriculum Coverage through the provocations suggested for Teeny tiny

Full version of KS1 PoS on pages 69-74
Photopcopiable version on page 8

Literacy	Lit 1 speak	Lit 2 listen	Lit 3 group	Lit 4 drama	Lit 5 word	Lit 6 spell	Lit 7 text1	Lit 8 text2	Lit 9 text3	Lit10 text4	Lit11 sentence	Lit12 presentation
	1.1	2.1	3.1	4.1	5.1	6.1	7.1	8.1	9.1	10.1	11.1	12.1
	1.2	2.2	3.2	4.2	5.2	6.2	7.2	8.2	9.2	10.2	11.2	12.2

Numeracy	Num 1 U&A	Num 2 count	Num 3 number	Num 4 calculate	Num 5 shape	Num 6 measure	Num 7 data
	1.1	2.1	3.1	4.1	5.1	6.1	7.1
	1.2	2.2	3.2	4.2	5.2	6.2	7.2

Science	SC1 Enquiry			SC2 Life processes					SC3 Materials		SC4 Phys processes		
	Sc1.1	Sc1.2	Sc1.3	Sc2.1	Sc2.2	Sc2.3	Sc2.4	Sc2.5	Sc3.1	Sc3.2	Sc4.1	Sc4.2	Sc4.3
	1.1a	1.2a	1.3a	2.1a	2.2a	2.3a	2.4a	2.5a	3.1a	3.2a	4.1a	4.2a	4.3a
	1.1b	1.2b	1.3b	2.1b	2.2b	2.3b	2.4b	2.5b	3.1b	3.2b	4.1b	4.2b	4.3b
	1.1c	1.2c	1.3c	2.1c	2.2c	2.3c		2.5c	3.1c		4.1c	4.2c	4.3c
	1.1d				2.2d				3.1d				4.3d
					2.2e								
					2.2f								
					2.2g								

ICT	ICT 1 finding out		ICT 2 ideas	ICT 3 reviewing	ICT 4 breadth
	1.1a	1.2a	2a	3a	4a
	1.1b	1.2b	2b	3b	4b
	1.1c	1.2c	2c	3c	4c
		1.2d			

D&T	D&T 1 developing	D&T 2 tool use	D&T 3 evaluating	D&T 4 materials	D&T 5 breadth
	1a	2a	3a	4a	5a
	1b	2b	3b	4b	5b
	1c	2c			5c
	1d	2d			
	1e	2e			

History	H1 chronology	H2 events, people	H3 interpret	H4 enquire	H5 org & comm	H6 breadth
	1a	2a	3a	4a	5a	6a
	1b	2b		4b		6b
						6c
						6d

Geography	G1.1 & G1.2 enquiry		G2 places	G3 processes	G4 environment	G5 breadth
	1.1a	1.2a	2a	3a	4a	5a
	1.1b	1.2b	2b	3b	4b	5b
	1.1c	1.2c	2c			5c
	1.1d	1.2d	2d			5d
			2e			

Music	M1 performing	M2 composing	M3 appraising	M4 listening	M5 breadth
	1a	2a	3a	4a	5a
	1b	2b	3b	4b	5b
	1c			4c	5c
					5d

PHSE & C	PSHEC1 conf & resp	PSHEC2 citizenship	PSHEC3 health	PSHEC4 relationships
	1a	2a	3a	4a
	1b	2b	3b	4b
	1c	2c	3c	4c
	1d	2d	3d	4d
	1e	2e	3e	4e
		2f	3f	
		2g	3g	
		2h		

Art & Design	A&D1 ideas	A&D2 making	A&D3 evaluating	A&D4 materials	A&D5 breadth
	1a	2a	3a	4a	5a
	1b	2b	3b	4b	5b
		2c		4c	5c
					5d

PE	PE1 devel skills	PE2 apply skills	PE3 evaluate	PE4 fitness	PE5 breadth
	1a	2a	3a	4a	5a dance
	1b	2b	3b	4b	5b games
		2c	3c		5c gym

Critical skills	Thinking Skills
problem solving	observing
decision making	classifying
critical thinking	prediction
creative thinking	making inferences
communication	problem solving
organisation	drawing conclusions
management	
leadership	

Coloured sand

Coloured sand

Previous experience in the Foundation Stage

Children will have had wide experience of pouring and sieving dry sand. They should have experimented with filling, emptying and moving sand in:

* free play with indoors and outside, with and without tools.

They may also have worked with other dry materials such as:

* soil;
* peat;
* bark;
* rice;
* glitter;
* flour;
* grass seed;

* grit;
* compost;
* gravel;
* lentils;
* salt;
* beans;
* small beads.

Pause for thought

In the early stages of working with these materials it is crucial to continue to observe the children. Only by doing this can you set developmentally appropriate challenges and provocations. The ideas listed here are offered as suggestions; the most exciting challenges will arise from children's own interests and motivations, which will only become apparent as you spend time with them, watching and joining them in their play. As you do this, you will be moving between the three interconnecting roles of observer, co-player, extender described below, and will be able to decide what you need to do next to take the learning forward.

The responsive adult (see page 5)

In three interconnecting roles, the responsive adult will be:

* observing
* listening
* interpreting

observer

* **modelling**
* **playing alongside**
* **offering suggestions**
* **responding sensitively**
* **initiating with care!**

co-player

* discussing ideas
* sharing thinking
* modelling new skills
* asking open questions
* being an informed extender
* instigating ideas & thoughts
* supporting children as they make links in learning
* making possibilities evident
* introducing new ideas and resources
* offering challenges and provocations

extender

Offering challenges and provocations - some ideas:

Colouring sand may be a new experience in itself. Allow plenty of time for experimenting with colouring the sand, and free play before embarking on challenges.

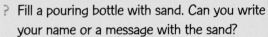

? Fill a pouring bottle with sand. Can you write your name or a message with the sand?

? Can you make a permanent picture by using sticky-backed plastic? Fix the plastic down (sticky side up) using Blutack.

? Can you design and make a repeating sand pattern with different colours and shapes? You could use spoons, pouring bottles, shakers or just your hands to make the patterns. You could try drawing the design on paper and pouring the sand into the design.

? Can you make a template or stencil for making repeating patterns?

? Make more patterns with zigzags, circles, lines, crosses of different colours. Try pouring sand onto perspex or glass, so you can see right through the patterns you make.

? Find some other small objects to add to the sand or to your pictures. Glitter, rice, gravel, sequins all work well.

? Use coloured sand and other objects to make a portrait of a friend. Take a photo to preserve your picture.

? Use the coloured sand to make mountains, valleys and dunes. Add some animals or vehicles to your landscape.

? Find a small container with different colours of sand so it makes layers. How can you fill the layers of different coloured sand so they don't mix up? (look at Google 'sandlady' for some ideas).

? Find a straw. Can you make patterns by blowing gently at the sand with the straw? Be careful when you blow, so the sand doesn't get in your eyes. What is the best distance to blow from to make a controlled line?

Ready for more?

- Explore pouring sand onto different sorts of papers, card and wallpaper. Try to get some embossed paper samples to try. How does the sand behave on different papers? Record what happens with a camera or on a chart.

- Devise some different containers for pouring sand. Try different shapes, sizes, numbers of holes. Use recycled containers, such as water bottles, cans or juice boxes.

- Can you find some different ways of making coloured sand? Which way is best? Make a sand recipe book for all the different kinds, so your friends can make them too.

- Can you make a maze or labrynth by pouring sand, or by making paths through a tray of sand?

- Put the word 'aboriginal art' or 'mandala' in Google Images. Can you make some sand patterns and pictures like this?

- Experiment with adding other things to the sand. Try seeds, lentils, gravel, small beads etc. How can you make the sand flow more quickly? ... more slowly? How can you make it pile up higher?

- Use string and glue to make a pattern on wood or card, then pour sand over to make embossed patterns.

- Make glue patterns on card, then pour sand over before it dries. Tip off the extra sand to reveal your picture or pattern.

Materials, equipment suppliers, websites, books and other references

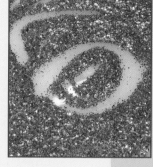

Suppliers of equipment and resources:

Coloured sand is available from lots of suppliers, just Google 'coloured sand' to get hundreds of addresses. Here are a few:

Sand in lots of colours, bottles and gems to hide are available from www.crazysand.co.uk

Gravel, coloured sand and aggregates (not fine sand) from www.rista.co.uk

All sorts of sand bottles from www.sandlady.co.uk

For a good range of colours in shaker bottles at a reasonable price try www.crafty-devils.com

You could make your own coloured sands by using silver sand, colouring it with food colouring or paint and drying it in a warm oven or the sun. **Don't dry it in a microwave, it will explode and do terminal damage to the microwave!!!**

TTS Group sell food colouring in bargain sized bottles www.tts-group.co.uk

ASCO www.ascoeducational.co.uk have glitter in big bottles with shakers. Or use salt pots, plastic ketchup or mustard bottles, cooking oil containers or just plastic water bottles with a hole poked in the top for drizzling and pouring sand onto trays or paper.

Ask for wallpaper sample books or ends of rolls from decorators or DIY stores.

For images of coloured sand and cliffs, try **Google Images** 'alum bay sands' 'coloured sand' 'sand art' 'sand cliffs' 'sand erosion' 'sand cliff erosion' 'glass makers'.

Pictures of the Isle of Wight and Alum Bay www.soton.ac.uk

Pictures of erosion of sand cliffs www.stacey.peak-media.co.uk/IoW/IsleofWight

The site of a glass manufacture on the isle of Wight www.wightonline.co.uk/alumbayglass

Some Books:

Sand Art; Top That Publishing (KIT and ideas)

Art from Sand and Earth; Gillian Chapman; Hodder Wayland

Sand to Glass Welcome Books: How Things are Made; Inez Snyder; Children's Press

Sand Art; Cheryl Owen; Walter Foster.

Curriculum coverage grid overleaf

Potential NC KS1 Curriculum Coverage through the provocations suggested for coloured sand

Literacy

	Lit 1 speak	Lit 2 listen	Lit 3 group	Lit 4 drama	Lit 5 word	Lit 6 spell	Lit 7 text1	Lit 8 text2	Lit 9 text3	Lit10 text4	Lit11 sentence	Lit12 presentation
Literacy	1.1	2.1	3.1	4.1	5.1	6.1	7.1	8.1	9.1	10.1	11.1	12.1
	1.2	2.2	3.2	4.2	5.2	6.2	7.2	8.2	9.2	10.2	11.2	12.2

Numeracy

	Num 1 U&A	Num 2 count	Num 3 number	Num 4 calculate	Num 5 shape	Num 6 measure	Num 7 data
Numeracy	1.1	2.1	3.1	4.1	5.1	6.1	7.1
	1.2	2.2	3.2	4.2	5.2	6.2	7.2

Full version of KS1 PoS on pages 69-74
Photopcopiable version on page 8

Science

	SC1 Enquiry			SC2 Life processes					SC3 Materials		SC4 Phys processes		
	Sc1.1	Sc1.2	Sc1.3	Sc2.1	Sc2.2	Sc2.3	Sc2.4	Sc2.5	Sc3.1	Sc3.2	Sc4.1	Sc4.2	Sc4.3
Science	1.1a	1.2a	1.3a	2.1a	2.2a	2.3a	2.4a	2.5a	3.1a	3.2a	4.1a	4.2a	4.3a
	1.1b	1.2b	1.3b	2.1b	2.2b	2.3b	2.4b	2.5b	3.1b	3.2b	4.1b	4.2b	4.3b
	1.1c	1.2c	1.3c	2.1c	2.2c	2.3c		2.5c	3.1c		4.1c	4.2c	4.3c
	1.1d				2.2d				3.1d				4.3d
					2.2e								
					2.2f								
					2.2g								

ICT

	ICT 1 finding out		ICT 2 ideas	ICT 3 reviewing	ICT 4 breadth
ICT	1.1a	1.2a	2a	3a	4a
	1.1b	1.2b	2b	3b	4b
	1.1c	1.2c	2c	3c	4c
		1.2d			

History

	H1 chronology	H2 events, people	H3 interpret	H4 enquire	H5 org & comm	H6 breadth
History	1a	2a	3a	4a	5a	6a
	1b	2b		4b		6b
						6c
						6d

Geography

	G1.1 & G1.2 enquiry		G2 places	G3 processes	G4 environment	G5 breadth
Geography	1.1a	1.2a	2a	3a	4a	5a
	1.1b	1.2b	2b	3b	4b	5b
	1.1c	1.2c	2c			5c
	1.1d	1.2d	2d			5d
			2e			

D&T

	D&T 1 developing	D&T 2 tool use	D&T 3 evaluating	D&T 4 materials	D&T 5 breadth
D&T	1a	2a	3a	4a	5a
	1b	2b	3b	4b	5b
	1c	2c			5c
	1d	2d			
	1e	2e			

Music

	M1 performing	M2 composing	M3 appraising	M4 listening	M5 breadth
Music	1a	2a	3a	4a	5a
	1b	2b	3b	4b	5b
	1c			4c	5c
					5d

PHSE & C

	PSHEC1 conf & resp	PSHEC2 citizenship	PSHEC3 health	PSHEC4 relationships
PHSE & C	1a	2a	3a	4a
	1b	2b	3b	4b
	1c	2c	3c	4c
	1d	2d	3d	4d
	1e	2e	3e	4e
		2f	3f	
		2g	3g	
		2h		

Art & Design

	A&D1 ideas	A&D2 making	A&D3 evaluating	A&D4 materials	A&D5 breadth
Art & Design	1a	2a	3a	4a	5a
	1b	2b	3b	4b	5b
		2c		4c	5c
					5d

PE

	PE1 devel skills	PE2 apply skills	PE3 evaluate	PE4 fitness	PE5 breadth
PE	1a	2a	3a	4a	5a dance
	1b	2b	3b	4b	5b games
		2c	3c		5c gym

Critical skills	Thinking Skills
problem solving	observing
decision making	classifying
critical thinking	prediction
creative thinking	making inferences
communication	problem solving
organisation	drawing conclusions
management	
leadership	

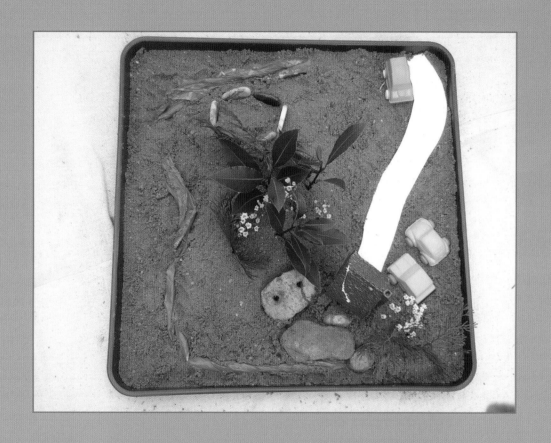

Maps and landscapes

Maps and landscapes

Previous experience in the Foundation Stage

Very young children need practice in being able to see two dimensional representations of landscapes. making 3D maps and landscapes helps with this, and children may have been involved in

* free play indoors and out of doors;
* combining maps with miniatures - figures, buildings, vehicles;
* using play mats of streets, cities, airports, harbours;
* sharing stories where maps and plans appear;
* drawing routes from home, plans of familiar places;
* looking at maps, plans, atlases, diagrams;
* looking for local features on walks and visits.

Pause for thought

In the early stages of working with these materials it is crucial to continue to observe the children. Only by doing this can you set developmentally appropriate challenges and provocations. The ideas listed here are offered as suggestions; the most exciting challenges will arise from children's own interests and motivations, which will only become apparent as you spend time with them, watching and joining them in their play. As you do this, you will be moving between the three interconnecting roles of observer, co-player, extender described below, and will be able to decide what you need to do next to take the learning forward.

The responsive adult (see page 5)

In three interconnecting roles, the responsive adult will be:

observer

* observing
* listening
* interpreting

co-player

* **modelling**
* **playing alongside**
* **offering suggestions**
* **responding sensitively**
* **initiating with care!**

extender

* discussing ideas
* sharing thinking
* modelling new skills
* asking open questions
* being an informed extender
* instigating ideas & thoughts
* supporting children as they make links in learning
* making possibilities evident
* introducing new ideas and resources
* offering challenges and provocations

Offering challenges and provocations - some ideas:

NOTE: Encourage children to add objects and materials to sand for these activities. They may need some ideas from you to get them started. Encourage them to collect natural materials and bring things from home to add to their creations.

? Can you make a map of your way to school, using sand, stones, gravel and bricks?

? Can you make a map of the school, with your classroom, the hall, the playground and the garden or field?

? Use sand, stones, gravel, leaves and other objects to make a garden. It can be a real one or an imaginary one.

? Choose a story that you like. Now make a landscape for part of the story. You could make some characters as well as a scene or map.

? Could you use some foil, sand and crumpled paper to make a moon map?

? Can you make a map of a beach with sea, a pier, some boats and other seaside things?

? Use sand, stones, boxes, small bricks, plastic, fabric, leaves and twigs to make a dinosaur landscape with small world dinosaurs and prehistoric trees; or a jungle landscape with animals, plants and a river; or a medieval landscape with a castle, knights and horses, a moat and a forest.

? Make a treasure island in the sand. Find some twigs and leaves for trees, make a lake or pond, bury a treasure and draw a treasure map so your friends can hunt for the treasure.

? Can you make an island surrounded by water? Think about it before you start, so you don't flood the classroom!

? Make a replica of your own garden with sand, gravel and stones? Use a box to make your house.

Ready for more?

- Work with some friends to make a bigger landscape or aerial views of real places. Try an airport, a building site, a space launch pad, a motorway, a safari park, a fairground or a farm. Use Google to find pictures and other information to help you.

- Try making bigger fantasy landscapes. You could design these together and then share the work of making them. How about a fantasy school, a park with new sorts of rides and equipment, a prehistoric theme park, an adventure land, a new planet or a castle just for kids.

- Look in Yellow Pages and ring or write to some local architects and builders. Ask them if they could come and talk about how they make plans and design new buildings and developments. They might let you have some real plans and maps to use.

- Find a map, a globe or an atlas and choose a country. Make a map of the country you choose. If you use a blue cloth for the sea it will be more realistic. Make the mountains, beaches and towns, using your own ideas for different parts and surfaces. You could work on your own or with friends.

- Find some model railway websites and request some catalogues for ideas for landscapes and models to make yourselves.

Materials, equipment suppliers, websites, books and other references

You will almost certainly have maps and atlases in school. Try to get some aerial photos of the area, or take photos of model layouts the children make. Make a map book of children's routes to school, the school plans, the way to get to local places. Some websites for aerial photos are:
www.earth.google.com a site for seeing everywhere, but a bit difficult to use
www.multimap.com and click on aerial photos for some free examples to look at
www.ukaerialphotos.com and click on Gallery for some example images of theme parks, bridges, sports stadiums etc.
www.tiscali.co.uk/travel/maps/aerialphotos click on 'aerial photos' and put in a post code, www.webbaviation.co.uk for county by county aerial photos, www.maps.google.co.uk will give you maps of anywhere by postcode, address, street name or locality. So will www.streetmap.co.uk, and www.ordnancesurvey.co.uk (maps of the UK) www.wildgoose.ac have aerial photos, maps and a range of other geographical resources.
For **miniature equipment such as buildings, people and other objects** use Lego, Playmobil and other small world models already in your school or try:
www.asco.co.uk for a set of City Blocks - wooden models of houses and other buildings
www.toypost.co.uk for a Little Wooden Village and Little Wooden Farm
www.gltc.co.uk (Great Little Trading Company) for Garage Town, Pirate Island, Metropolis Train sets.Shops, websites & catalogues for model train enthusiasts will provide people, animals, vehicles, trees, bushes, fences and other objects in a range of different scales for perfectionists!
Google Images 'model' 'miniature' 'train set' 'aerial view' 'architectural models' the last one has some very interesting images!

Some Books and stories about maps:
There's a Map on My Lap! All about Maps; Tish Rabe; Random House
As the Crow Flies: A First Book of Maps; Gail Hartman; Athaeneum Books
Buried Blueprints; maps of lost worlds; Albert Lorenz; Harry Abrahams
Looking at Maps and Globes; Carmen Bredeson; Children's Press
Mapping Penny's World; Loreen Leedy; Henry Holt
Rosie's Walk; Pat Hutchens; Scholastic.

Curriculum coverage grid overleaf

Potential NC KS1 Curriculum Coverage through the provocations suggested for maps and landscapes

Full version of KS1 PoS on pages 69-74
Photopcopiable version on page 8

Literacy

	Lit 1 speak	Lit 2 listen	Lit 3 group	Lit 4 drama	Lit 5 word	Lit 6 spell	Lit 7 text1	Lit 8 text2	Lit 9 text3	Lit10 text4	Lit11 sentence	Lit12 presentation
Literacy	1.1	2.1	3.1	4.1	5.1	6.1	7.1	8.1	9.1	10.1	11.1	12.1
	1.2	2.2	3.2	4.2	5.2	6.2	7.2	8.2	9.2	10.2	11.2	12.2

Numeracy

	Num 1 U&A	Num 2 count	Num 3 number	Num 4 calculate	Num 5 shape	Num 6 measure	Num 7 data
Numeracy	1.1	2.1	3.1	4.1	5.1	6.1	7.1
	1.2	2.2	3.2	4.2	5.2	6.2	7.2

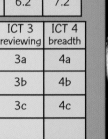

NASA web

Science

	SC1 Enquiry			SC2 Life processes					SC3 Materials		SC4 Phys processes		
	Sc1.1	Sc1.2	Sc1.3	Sc2.1	Sc2.2	Sc2.3	Sc2.4	Sc2.5	Sc3.1	Sc3.2	Sc4.1	Sc4.2	Sc4.3
Science	1.1a	1.2a	1.3a	2.1a	2.2a	2.3a	2.4a	2.5a	3.1a	3.2a	4.1a	4.2a	4.3a
	1.1b	1.2b	1.3b	2.1b	2.2b	2.3b	2.4b	2.5b	3.1b	3.2b	4.1b	4.2b	4.3b
	1.1c	1.2c	1.3c	2.1c	2.2c	2.3c		2.5c	3.1c		4.1c	4.2c	4.3c
	1.1d				2.2d				3.1d				4.3d
					2.2e								
					2.2f								
					2.2g								

ICT

	ICT 1 finding out		ICT 2 ideas	ICT 3 reviewing	ICT 4 breadth
	1.1a	1.2a	2a	3a	4a
ICT	1.1b	1.2b	2b	3b	4b
	1.1c	1.2c	2c	3c	4c
		1.2d			

D&T

	D&T 1 developing	D&T 2 tool use	D&T 3 evaluating	D&T 4 materials	D&T 5 breadth
	1a	2a	3a	4a	5a
D&T	1b	2b	3b	4b	5b
	1c	2c			5c
	1d	2d			
	1e	2e			

History

	H1 chronology	H2 events, people	H3 interpret	H4 enquire	H5 org & comm	H6 breadth
	1a	2a	3a	4a	5a	6a
History	1b	2b		4b		6b
						6c
						6d

Geography

	G1.1 & G1.2 enquiry		G2 places	G3 processes	G4 environment	G5 breadth
	1.1a	1.2a	2a	3a	4a	5a
Geography	1.1b	1.2b	2b	3b	4b	5b
	1.1c	1.2c	2c			5c
	1.1d	1.2d	2d			5d
			2e			

Music

	M1 performing	M2 composing	M3 appraising	M4 listening	M5 breadth
	1a	2a	3a	4a	5a
Music	1b	2b	3b	4b	5b
	1c			4c	5c
					5d

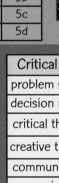

PHSE & C

	PSHEC1 conf & resp	PSHEC2 citizenship	PSHEC3 health	PSHEC4 relationships
	1a	2a	3a	4a
	1b	2b	3b	4b
PHSE & C	1c	2c	3c	4c
	1d	2d	3d	4d
	1e	2e	3e	4e
		2f	3f	
		2g	3g	
		2h		

Art & Design

	A&D1 ideas	A&D2 making	A&D3 evaluating	A&D4 materials	A&D5 breadth
	1a	2a	3a	4a	5a
Art & Design	1b	2b	3b	4b	5b
		2c		4c	5c
					5d

PE

	PE1 devel skills	PE2 apply skills	PE3 evaluate	PE4 fitness	PE5 breadth
	1a	2a	3a	4a	5a dance
PE	1b	2b	3b	4b	5b games
		2c	3c		5c gym

Photo copyright ASCO

Critical skills	Thinking Skills
problem solving	observing
decision making	classifying
critical thinking	prediction
creative thinking	making inferences
communication	problem solving
organisation	drawing conclusions
management	
leadership	

Diggers and excavators

Diggers and excavators

Previous experience in the Foundation Stage

Most children, and particularly boys, will have had experience of using plastic or metal diggers, dump trucks, tipper lorries and other construction vehicles in sand, gravel and mud. They will probably have used them:

* in trays with sand, compost, mud;
* in free play indoors and outside;
* for scooping gravel or stones;
* with small world people in construction play;
* for solving spatial problems and building structures;
* with logs, sticks and stones to make scenes and environments;
* in role play, while wearing construction worker hats and clothes.

Pause for thought

In the early stages of working with these materials it is crucial to continue to observe the children. Only by doing this can you set developmentally appropriate challenges and provocations. The ideas listed here are offered as suggestions; the most exciting challenges will arise from children's own interests and motivations, which will only become apparent as you spend time with them, watching and joining them in their play. As you do this, you will be moving between the three interconnecting roles of observer, co-player, extender described below, and will be able to decide what you need to do next to take the learning forward.

The responsive adult (see page 5)

In three interconnecting roles, the responsive adult will be:

* observing
* listening
* interpreting

observer

* **modelling**
* **playing alongside**
* **offering suggestions**
* **responding sensitively**
* **initiating with care!**

co-player

* discussing ideas
* sharing thinking
* modelling new skills
* asking open questions
* being an informed extender
* instigating ideas & thoughts
* supporting children as they make links in learning
* making possibilities evident
* introducing new ideas and resources
* offering challenges and provocations

extender

Offering challenges and provocations - some ideas:

? Find out how all the diggers work, talk about their best features and choose a favourite to work with as you scoop and move sand or gravel.

? Use the diggers to make tracks in the sand. Take some photos of the different tracks they make.

? Can you use your favourite digger to scoop all the sand into one big pile, without using your hands?

? Practice tipping loads of sand from the tipper lorries, using the mechanisms on the toy.

? Can you use the diggers and trucks to make an absolutely smooth road across the sand tray? How did you do it?

? Put 'digger' in Google Images and in Google web, and see what you find. E-mail some digger firms for some leaflets.

? Take the diggers outside and see how well they work with mud or compost. Which one works best? Record your findings with photos or a chart.

? Look out for construction sites when you are out with your family. Watch what diggers do and how they move. Look at what happens when they go backwards. Take some photos if you can and bring them to school for reference when you are working with the sand.

? Use sand and different gravels with diggers. Look at how they move and scoop. Which materials are easiest to work with?

? Add some branches and small logs to the sand and make some mounds and caves with the diggers.

? Pile the sand up and find the best way to make tunnels in the sand, just using toy diggers. Take photos of the best ones. Now look on the internet for the way tunnels are made in real life.

Ready for more?

- Can you design a digger scoop and build it in junk materials - look at some sand scoops for ideas. Test your scoops with real sand and evaluate their strengths and weaknesses.

- Use photos or film of diggers and other construction vehicles to make a Power Point presentation, a book or a video of how they work, or a construction story.

- Look on educational suppliers sites and see if you can find out about working diggers that kids can ride on. Get some catalogues or other information.

- Contact a local construction firm and ask if they would bring a digger to school so you can look at it safely, take photos and ask questions.

- Look in your library or a public library for books and stories about construction machinery. Can you find out about the biggest digger in the world? Write up how you found your information, so other people can find out too.

- Look at www.diggerland.com where you can download photos of all sorts of diggers and print them off. You can also request a brochure. When you have some information, make a display with a sand tray and toy diggers in front, and your pictures, photos and other information behind them. Make signs and labels and introduce your display to your class.

Materials, equipment suppliers, websites, books and other references

There are hundreds of different toy diggers in many different sizes. Try putting 'toy digger' in Google Images to find a long, long list of different diggers from the small, accurate die cast models supplied by Corgi and other toy manufacturers.

See Caterpillar construction machines at www.cat.com and click through to the shop for die cast construction models.

Or www.hyundai.be/news/products/big-float-prefers-hyundai to look at diggers that float.

Or look at www.virtualquarry.co.uk (this needs a media player to look at a quarry at work).

The British geological Survey site www.bgs.ac.uk has geological maps and photos.

Google Images responds well to 'quarry', 'digger', 'sand', and some inspiration may come by trying 'scoop', 'sandpile', 'dune', 'sand cliff'. Also try some of these in www.wikipedia.org to get reference material and pictures.

Or try www.worsleyschool.net for their pictures of huge excavators.

www.diggerland.com is an adventure park where children can ride and drive diggers.

Some books:

Mike Mulligan and His Steam Shovel; Virginia Lee Burton; Frances Lincoln (a long time favourite story)

Are you my Mother?; P D Eastman; Harper Collins (a baby bird falls from the nest and is eventually returned to its mother by a digger)

Dazzling Diggers; Tody Mitton; Kingfisher Books

Diggers and Cranes; Caroline Young; Usborne

Diggers and Cranes; Jim Pipe; Franklin Watts

Drawing Trucks and Diggers; Caterpillar

Wild About Trucks and Diggers; Caroline Bingham; Ticktock media

and of course there is Bob the Builder!

DVD:

Big Machines 1 - Diggers And Dumpers

Let's Look At Diggers

Ready 2 Learn - Diggers And Dumpers.

Curriculum coverage grid overleaf

Full version of KS1 PoS on pages 69-74
Photocopiable version on page 8

Literacy

	Lit 1 speak	Lit 2 listen	Lit 3 group	Lit 4 drama	Lit 5 word	Lit 6 spell	Lit 7 text1	Lit 8 text2	Lit 9 text3	Lit10 text4	Lit11 sentence	Lit12 presentation
	1.1	2.1	3.1	4.1	5.1	6.1	7.1	8.1	9.1	10.1	11.1	12.1
	1.2	2.2	3.2	4.2	5.2	6.2	7.2	8.2	9.2	10.2	11.2	12.2

Numeracy

	Num 1 U&A	Num 2 count	Num 3 number	Num 4 calculate	Num 5 shape	Num 6 measure	Num 7 data
	1.1	2.1	3.1	4.1	5.1	6.1	7.1
	1.2	2.2	3.2	4.2	5.2	6.2	7.2

Science

	SC1 Enquiry			SC2 Life processes					SC3 Materials		SC4 Phys processes		
	Sc1.1	Sc1.2	Sc1.3	Sc2.1	Sc2.2	Sc2.3	Sc2.4	Sc2.5	Sc3.1	Sc3.2	Sc4.1	Sc4.2	Sc4.3
	1.1a	1.2a	1.3a	2.1a	2.2a	2.3a	2.4a	2.5a	3.1a	3.2a	4.1a	4.2a	4.3a
	1.1b	1.2b	1.3b	2.1b	2.2b	2.3b	2.4b	2.5b	3.1b	3.2b	4.1b	4.2b	4.3b
	1.1c	1.2c	1.3c	2.1c	2.2c	2.3c		2.5c	3.1c		4.1c	4.2c	4.3c
	1.1d				2.2d				3.1d				4.3d
					2.2e								
					2.2f								
					2.2g								

ICT

	ICT 1 finding out		ICT 2 ideas	ICT 3 reviewing	ICT 4 breadth
	1.1a	1.2a	2a	3a	4a
	1.1b	1.2b	2b	3b	4b
	1.1c	1.2c	2c	3c	4c
		1.2d			

D&T

	D&T 1 developing	D&T 2 tool use	D&T 3 evaluating	D&T 4 materials	D&T 5 breadth
	1a	2a	3a	4a	5a
	1b	2b	3b	4b	5b
	1c	2c			5c
	1d	2d			
	1e	2e			

History

	H1 chronology	H2 events, people	H3 interpret	H4 enquire	H5 org & comm	H6 breadth
	1a	2a	3a	4a	5a	6a
	1b	2b		4b		6b
						6c
						6d

Geography

	G1.1 & G1.2 enquiry		G2 places	G3 processes	G4 environment	G5 breadth
	1.1a	1.2a	2a	3a	4a	5a
	1.1b	1.2b	2b	3b	4b	5b
	1.1c	1.2c	2c			5c
	1.1d	1.2d	2d			5d
			2e			

Music

	M1 performing	M2 composing	M3 appraising	M4 listening	M5 breadth
	1a	2a	3a	4a	5a
	1b	2b	3b	4b	5b
	1c			4c	5c
					5d

PHSE & C

	PSHEC1 conf & resp	PSHEC2 citizenship	PSHEC3 health	PSHEC4 relationships
	1a	2a	3a	4a
	1b	2b	3b	4b
	1c	2c	3c	4c
	1d	2d	3d	4d
	1e	2e	3e	4e
		2f	3f	
		2g	3g	
		2h		

Art & Design

	A&D1 ideas	A&D2 making	A&D3 evaluating	A&D4 materials	A&D5 breadth
	1a	2a	3a	4a	5a
	1b	2b	3b	4b	5b
		2c		4c	5c
					5d

PE

	PE1 devel skills	PE2 apply skills	PE3 evaluate	PE4 fitness	PE5 breadth
	1a	2a	3a	4a	5a dance
	1b	2b	3b	4b	5b games
		2c	3c		5c gym

Critical skills	Thinking Skills
problem solving	observing
decision making	classifying
critical thinking	prediction
creative thinking	making inferences
communication	problem solving
organisation	drawing conclusions
management	
leadership	

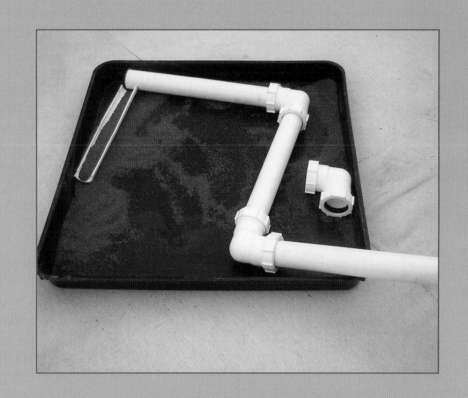

Drainpipes and guttering

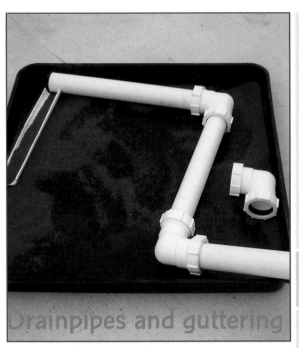

Drainpipes and guttering

Previous experience in the Foundation Stage

Drainpipes, guttering and other plumbing materials are easily available from DIY superstores and can be used to enhance many kinds of play and investigation. Children may already have had experience of these materials in the Foundation Stage:

* in free play indoors and outside;
* in sand and water play;
* combined with small world figured to make bridges and tunnels;
* to balance and build, exploring abstract and imaginative constructions;
* combined with malleable materials such as dough, gloop, foam, clay, mud;
* to explore sliding, rolling, pouring and filling with toy cars, objects, abstract shapes, natural materials such as stones, seeds etc.

Pause for thought

In the early stages of working with these materials it is crucial to continue to observe the children. Only by doing this can you set developmentally appropriate challenges and provocations. The ideas listed here are offered as suggestions; the most exciting challenges will arise from children's own interests and motivations, which will only become apparent as you spend time with them, watching and joining them in their play. As you do this, you will be moving between the three interconnecting roles of observer, co-player, extender described below, and will be able to decide what you need to do next to take the learning forward.

The responsive adult (see page 5)

In three interconnecting roles, the responsive adult will be:

observer

* observing
* listening
* interpreting

co-player

* **modelling**
* **playing alongside**
* **offering suggestions**
* **responding sensitively**
* **initiating with care!**

extender

* discussing ideas
* sharing thinking
* modelling new skills
* asking open questions
* being an informed extender
* instigating ideas & thoughts
* supporting children as they make links in learning
* making possibilities evident
* introducing new ideas and resources
* offering challenges and provocations

Offering challenges and provocations - some ideas:

? Can you join (X) number of pieces of pipe together to make an interesting shape to pour sand through?

? What is the longest sand run of pipes and guttering you can make? Can you get sand to move all the way along it?

? How can you get sand to flow round corners?

? How many different ways can you find to join 4/5/6 pieces of pipe or guttering together?

? Can you make a marble run with sand, pipes, tape and guttering?

? Can you find a way to make sand run through a pipe without tilting it?

? Try using lentils, grass seed, bird food or dried peas instead of sand. Do these move through the pipes more easily? Which one is best? Take some photos of your experiments.

? Can you cut and join a series of empty plastic bottles together to make your own drainpipe?

? Go for a walk round your school and make drawings of the different ways that pipes, guttering and plumbing pipes are used. Look for the different joins between pipes. Look under sinks, outside, under the edges of the roof, and near radiators.

? On a rainy day, watch the gutters and rainpipes round your school. Does anything else apart from water come out? How could you catch some of the things that get washed down?

? Find or make some small pipes or pieces of tubing. Can you use these to fill toy trucks with sand and gravel? How can you steady the little pipes so the sand goes into the truck when you are using your hands to pour with?

Ready for more?

- Try joining pipes together with different materials - duct tape, fabric, sellotape, Blutak. Which works best? Record what you find out, using a camera, clipboard, database or chart.

- Collect or make some pipes and tubes of different diameters and materials. Test them to find which ones work best for moving sand.

- Add some figures or animals to the sand and see if you can move them through your constructions.

- Can you find a way to support the guttering and pipes so the sand can flow downhill.

- Can you build a sand cascade?

- Can you fix 2 or 3 pipes together in a bunch so you can fill containers more quickly?

- Put 'Pompidou' in Google images for pictures of plumbing on the outside of buildings.

- Can you make a sand 'shower head' like a water shower?

- Make the longest length of pipe you can by fixing drainpipes together. It may be easier to do this outside. Now explore different ways of making the pipe slope by propping the end up. Send sand, gravel, stones or beads down the long pipe. Which angle is best for making sure all the sand comes out at the end? Which angle makes the sand run fastest?

Materials, equipment, suppliers, websites, books and other references

The best value in guttering and drainpipes will be found locally at builders' merchants and DIY superstores. Get straight bits and some joints and bends. Flexible joints make good additions. Add some duct tape (the silver stuff), and try to get this at bargain or 'Pound' shops where it will be much cheaper.

If you can afford to buy something from an educational supplier, try the wooden viaduct from Asco www.ascoeducational.co.uk or TTS www.tts-group.co.uk who stock a bamboo water channelling kit which could be used for sand too. Many suppliers have sand wheels and marble runs of different sorts that can be added to guttering and pipes for more challenges. Add some tubing (available from DIY shops and builders' merchants). This works with sand too!

Local plumbers may respond to a letter from the children, and donate some of these resources, or there may be a parent of children in the school who has links with the building trade. Marble runs are good for sand too. You can get them from most educational suppliers, or toyshops, or make your own from cardboard tubes and guttering. The children may have to experiment with the slope of the runs to make the sand or gravel move, and you may want to add some small objects such as beads or pea gravel to sand to help the flow. www.rista.co.uk sell Diamonique beads in a range of colours, which might provide an alternative to sand.

Try **Google Images** 'Pompidou Centre' or 'Lloyd's building' to find pictures of two buildings with their plumbing on the outside. You could also try 'pipes', 'guttering', 'plumbing', 'water pipes', 'burst water main', 'tubing', 'fireman hose', 'garden hose', or **Google Web** 'plumbing', 'water pipes'.

Books:
A Day With a Plumber; Mark Thomas; Children's Press.

Curriculum coverage grid overleaf

Potential NC KS1 Curriculum Coverage through the provocations suggested for drainpipes and guttering

Full version of KS1 PoS on pages 69-74
Photocopiable version on page 8

Literacy

	Lit 1 speak	Lit 2 listen	Lit 3 group	Lit 4 drama	Lit 5 word	Lit 6 spell	Lit 7 text1	Lit 8 text2	Lit 9 text3	Lit10 text4	Lit11 sentence	Lit12 presentation
	1.1	2.1	3.1	4.1	5.1	6.1	7.1	8.1	9.1	10.1	11.1	12.1
	1.2	2.2	3.2	4.2	5.2	6.2	7.2	8.2	9.2	10.2	11.2	12.2

Numeracy

	Num 1 U&A	Num 2 count	Num 3 number	Num 4 calculate	Num 5 shape	Num 6 measure	Num 7 data
	1.1	2.1	3.1	4.1	5.1	6.1	7.1
	1.2	2.2	3.2	4.2	5.2	6.2	7.2

Science

	SC1 Enquiry			SC2 Life processes					SC3 Materials		SC4 Phys processes		
	Sc1.1	Sc1.2	Sc1.3	Sc2.1	Sc2.2	Sc2.3	Sc2.4	Sc2.5	Sc3.1	Sc3.2	Sc4.1	Sc4.2	Sc4.3
	1.1a	1.2a	1.3a	2.1a	2.2a	2.3a	2.4a	2.5a	3.1a	3.2a	4.1a	4.2a	4.3a
	1.1b	1.2b	1.3b	2.1b	2.2b	2.3b	2.4b	2.5b	3.1b	3.2b	4.1b	4.2b	4.3b
	1.1c	1.2c	1.3c	2.1c	2.2c	2.3c		2.5c	3.1c		4.1c	4.2c	4.3c
	1.1d				2.2d				3.1d				4.3d
					2.2e								
					2.2f								
					2.2g								

ICT

	ICT 1 finding out		ICT 2 ideas	ICT 3 reviewing	ICT 4 breadth
	1.1a	1.2a	2a	3a	4a
	1.1b	1.2b	2b	3b	4b
	1.1c	1.2c	2c	3c	4c
		1.2d			

History

	H1 chronology	H2 events, people	H3 interpret	H4 enquire	H5 org & comm	H6 breadth
	1a	2a	3a	4a	5a	6a
	1b	2b		4b		6b
						6c
						6d

D&T

	D&T 1 developing	D&T 2 tool use	D&T 3 evaluating	D&T 4 materials	D&T 5 breadth
	1a	2a	3a	4a	5a
	1b	2b	3b	4b	5b
	1c	2c			5c
	1d	2d			
	1e	2e			

Geography

	G1.1 & G1.2 enquiry		G2 places	G3 processes	G4 environment	G5 breadth
	1.1a	1.2a	2a	3a	4a	5a
	1.1b	1.2b	2b	3b	4b	5b
	1.1c	1.2c	2c			5c
	1.1d	1.2d	2d			5d
			2e			

Music

	M1 performing	M2 composing	M3 appraising	M4 listening	M5 breadth
	1a	2a	3a	4a	5a
	1b	2b	3b	4b	5b
	1c			4c	5c
					5d

PHSE & C

	PSHEC1 conf & resp	PSHEC2 citizenship	PSHEC3 health	PSHEC4 relationships
	1a	2a	3a	4a
	1b	2b	3b	4b
	1c	2c	3c	4c
	1d	2d	3d	4d
	1e	2e	3e	4e
		2f	3f	
		2g	3g	
		2h		

Art & Design

	A&D1 ideas	A&D2 making	A&D3 evaluating	A&D4 materials	A&D5 breadth
	1a	2a	3a	4a	5a
	1b	2b	3b	4b	5b
		2c		4c	5c
					5d

PE

	PE1 devel skills	PE2 apply skills	PE3 evaluate	PE4 fitness	PE5 breadth
	1a	2a	3a	4a	5a dance
	1b	2b	3b	4b	5b games
		2c	3c		5c gym

Critical skills	Thinking Skills
problem solving	observing
decision making	classifying
critical thinking	prediction
creative thinking	making inferences
communication	problem solving
organisation	drawing conclusions
management	
leadership	

Marks and patterns

Marks and patterns

Previous experience in the Foundation Stage

In the Foundation Stage, children will have had experience of mark making and patterning in a wide range of contexts and with different sorts of tools during both child initiated and adult directed learning:

* mark making in sand, mud, dough etc with hands, fingers, feet, and with tools like rakes, spades, forks;
* painting drawing and printing;
* patterning with pegboards and construction toys, shapes, bead threading etc;
* making rubbings of patterned and textured surfaces;
* working with 2D and 3D shapes;
* free access to a mark making area with a range of materials and tools.

Pause for thought

In the early stages of working with these materials it is crucial to continue to observe the children. Only by doing this can you set developmentally appropriate challenges and provocations. The ideas listed here are offered as suggestions; the most exciting challenges will arise from children's own interests and motivations, which will only become apparent as you spend time with them, watching and joining them in their play. As you do this, you will be moving between the three interconnecting roles of observer, co-player, extender described below, and will be able to decide what you need to do next to take the learning forward.

The responsive adult (see page 5)

In three interconnecting roles, the responsive adult will be:

observer

* observing
* listening
* interpreting

co-player

* **modelling**
* **playing alongside**
* **offering suggestions**
* **responding sensitively**
* **initiating with care!**

extender

* discussing ideas
* sharing thinking
* modelling new skills
* asking open questions
* being an informed extender
* instigating ideas & thoughts
* supporting children as they make links in learning
* making possibilities evident
* introducing new ideas and resources
* offering challenges and provocations

Offering challenges and provocations - some ideas:

? Use combs of different sizes and shapes to make patterns in dry and damp sand.

? Collect some natural or man-made objects and make some patterns in dry or damp sand. Try nuts, seeds, stones, plastic caps, sticks, shells, counters, coins, glass beads.

? Can you make your own combs from card, plastic or polystyrene for making patterns? Which material works best? Which is easiest to cut?

? Make some coloured sand for pouring and combing into patterns? Can you use more than one colour?

? Find some toy cars and trucks, and use them to make patterns in the sand.

? Use a collection of objects to make a pattern of marks in damp sand. Can your friend match the objects with the marks you have made?

? Write a rhyme, song or poem in the sand, using a salt pot or other pourer.

? Write a message in the sand and leave it where other people can read it. See if you get any replies!

? Copy a pattern or a picture with only one finger. Try with the other hand - is it harder? Now try writing with both hands together.

? Hide something in shallow sand and make tracks or footprints as clues for your friend to find what you have hidden.

? Paint a piece of card with a mixture of white glue and water. Now sprinkle sand or draw patterns with a sand pourer on the glue before it dries. What happens to your sand pattern when it is dry?

? Explore how you could use a sieve or colander to make sand patterns. What did you find out? Try using different sorts of containers with holes.

Ready for more?

- Bury wet paper or fabric in sand to make embossed patterns in damp sand.

- Use buttons, sequins, beads, Lego bits and other small objects to make patterns in dry or damp sand. Find the best way to get them out again when you have finished!

- Get everyone to write their name in wet sand, take some photos and make them into a calendar or a poster, or cards or gift tags.

- Make a word bank in the sand of all the words you can write. Take photos and make a display.

- Who can make the longest continuous line in the sand?

- Put some words in Google images (eg 'pattern' 'zigzag' 'stripes' 'animal print') and see if you can find some patterns to copy.

- Find a mark making tool and see how many marks you can make in a tray of sand - can you make 100? 200? 1000? 10,000?

- Use empty plastic bottles and some string to find out how to make patterns with sand. Make holes in plastic bottles and suspend them over a tray or black paper, so the sand can come out of the holes you have made. Try different numbers of holes, and watch to see if the pattern changes when you swing the bottle gently on the string.

Materials, equipment suppliers, websites, books and other references

Photo copyright ASCO

Suppliers: www.asco.co.uk for sand combs and rollers or TTS Group.

You can also use expired credit and store cards to make cheap combs for patterning. Just cut the edges with scissors to make different patterns. Or use stiff card or the plastic from milk and water bottles.

Pet combs and hair combs of all sorts will provide a source of different patterns (try Bargain and Pound shops for cheap versions).

Encourage children to collect sticks, twigs, old pencils, old toothbrushes and household tools for patterning.

Provide shallow trays (eg plant saucers, windowsill trays, builders' trays) of dry sand, which only need a finger to make patterns, pictures and letters!

www.creativekidsathome.com have free-to-download Mandala templates and photos of the activity.

Try Google Images: 'patterns sand', 'sand ripples', 'footprints', 'sand sculpture', 'fossil footprints'.

Some books:

Nature's Playground; Fiona Danks; Frances Lincoln

Pattern and Texture; and Colour; Paul Flux; Heinemann

Fun with Pattern and Shape; Jenny Ackland; Oxford University Press

Pattern; Henry Pluckrose; Franklin Watts

Patterns Everywhere; Julie Dalton; Children;s Press

Discover Science; Pattern; Kim Taylor; Chrysalis

Art from Sand and Earth; Gillian Chapman; Hodder Wayland

Mandala Colouring books; (you could use these as patterns for sand art); Monique Mandali; Mandali Publishing (available through Amazon)

Sand Paintings of the Navaho; Franc Johnson Newcomb; Dover Publications.

Curriculum coverage grid overleaf

Potential NC KS1 Curriculum Coverage through the provocations suggested for marks and patterns

Literacy	Lit 1 speak	Lit 2 listen	Lit 3 group	Lit 4 drama	Lit 5 word	Lit 6 spell	Lit 7 text1	Lit 8 text2	Lit 9 text3	Lit10 text4	Lit11 sentence	Lit12 presentation
	1.1	2.1	3.1	4.1	5.1	6.1	7.1	8.1	9.1	10.1	11.1	12.1
	1.2	2.2	3.2	4.2	5.2	6.2	7.2	8.2	9.2	10.2	11.2	12.2

Numeracy	Num 1 U&A	Num 2 count	Num 3 number	Num 4 calculate	Num 5 shape	Num 6 measure	Num 7 data
	1.1	2.1	3.1	4.1	5.1	6.1	7.1
	1.2	2.2	3.2	4.2	5.2	6.2	7.2

Full version of KS1 PoS on pages 69-74
Photopcopiable version on page 8

Science	SC1 Enquiry			SC2 Life processes					SC3 Materials		SC4 Phys processes		
	Sc1.1	Sc1.2	Sc1.3	Sc2.1	Sc2.2	Sc2.3	Sc2.4	Sc2.5	Sc3.1	Sc3.2	Sc4.1	Sc4.2	Sc4.3
	1.1a	1.2a	1.3a	2.1a	2.2a	2.3a	2.4a	2.5a	3.1a	3.2a	4.1a	4.2a	4.3a
	1.1b	1.2b	1.3b	2.1b	2.2b	2.3b	2.4b	2.5b	3.1b	3.2b	4.1b	4.2b	4.3b
	1.1c	1.2c	1.3c	2.1c	2.2c	2.3c		2.5c	3.1c		4.1c	4.2c	4.3c
	1.1d				2.2d				3.1d				4.3d
					2.2e								
					2.2f								
					2.2g								

ICT	ICT 1 finding out		ICT 2 ideas	ICT 3 reviewing	ICT 4 breadth
	1.1a	1.2a	2a	3a	4a
	1.1b	1.2b	2b	3b	4b
	1.1c	1.2c	2c	3c	4c
		1.2d			

D&T	D&T 1 developing	D&T 2 tool use	D&T 3 evaluating	D&T 4 materials	D&T 5 breadth
	1a	2a	3a	4a	5a
	1b	2b	3b	4b	5b
	1c	2c			5c
	1d	2d			
	1e	2e			

History	H1 chronology	H2 events, people	H3 interpret	H4 enquire	H5 org & comm	H6 breadth
	1a	2a	3a	4a	5a	6a
	1b	2b		4b		6b
						6c
						6d

Geography	G1.1 & G1.2 enquiry		G2 places	G3 processes	G4 environment	G5 breadth
	1.1a	1.2a	2a	3a	4a	5a
	1.1b	1.2b	2b	3b	4b	5b
	1.1c	1.2c	2c			5c
	1.1d	1.2d	2d			5d
			2e			

Music	M1 performing	M2 composing	M3 appraising	M4 listening	M5 breadth
	1a	2a	3a	4a	5a
	1b	2b	3b	4b	5b
	1c			4c	5c
					5d

PHSE & C	PSHEC1 conf & resp	PSHEC2 citizenship	PSHEC3 health	PSHEC4 relationships
	1a	2a	3a	4a
	1b	2b	3b	4b
	1c	2c	3c	4c
	1d	2d	3d	4d
	1e	2e	3e	4e
		2f	3f	
		2g	3g	
		2h		

Art & Design	A&D1 ideas	A&D2 making	A&D3 evaluating	A&D4 materials	A&D5 breadth
	1a	2a	3a	4a	5a
	1b	2b	3b	4b	5b
		2c		4c	5c
					5d

PE	PE1 devel skills	PE2 apply skills	PE3 evaluate	PE4 fitness	PE5 breadth
	1a	2a	3a	4a	5a dance
	1b	2b	3b	4b	5b games
		2c	3c		5c gym

Critical skills	Thinking Skills
problem solving	observing
decision making	classifying
critical thinking	prediction
creative thinking	making inferences
communication	problem solving
organisation	drawing conclusions
management	
leadership	

Photo copyright ASCO

Photo copyright ASCO

Photo copyright ASCO

Hide and find

Hide and find

Previous experience in the Foundation Stage

Hiding and treasure hunts are fascinating for children of all ages. In the Foundation Stage many children will have experienced adult and child devised hide-and-find games in:

* free play indoors and in the garden;
* in sand and other malleable materials;
* in more formal games such as Hunt the Thimble, Hunt the Teddy, Find the Object;
* in discussions relating to positional language (under, behind, in front, beside etc);
* making their own games of 'hide and find' or 'hide and seek' in their setting or at home;
* reading and talking about hidden treasure in stories, rhymes, films, TV stories and fact books.

Pause for thought

In the early stages of working with these materials it is crucial to continue to observe the children. Only by doing this can you set developmentally appropriate challenges and provocations. The ideas listed here are offered as suggestions; the most exciting challenges will arise from children's own interests and motivations, which will only become apparent as you spend time with them, watching and joining them in their play. As you do this, you will be moving between the three interconnecting roles of observer, co-player, extender described below, and will be able to decide what you need to do next to take the learning forward.

The responsive adult (see page 5)

In three interconnecting roles, the responsive adult will be:

* observing
* listening
* interpreting

observer

* **modelling**
* **playing alongside**
* **offering suggestions**
* **responding sensitively**
* **initiating with care!**

co-player

* discussing ideas
* sharing thinking
* modelling new skills
* asking open questions
* being an informed extender
* instigating ideas & thoughts
* supporting children as they make links in learning
* making possibilities evident
* introducing new ideas and resources
* offering challenges and provocations

extender

Offering challenges and provocations - some ideas:

? Make a list of some small objects. Now hide them in a box or bowl of sand for your friend to find and check off on the list.

? Hide lots of small objects in a big box of sand. Set some challenges to find specific things or numbers of things - 5 dinosaurs, 6 buttons, 8 keys, 3 crabs, 10 coins etc.

? Put lots of dried peas, marbles or grains of rice in a sand box. How many can you find? Can you work out a good way of counting these very small things?

? Bury some objects and write descriptions of them instead of a list - a green animal, a silver metal object etc. Challenge your friends to find them.

? Bury lots of objects, then make a graph of all the things you find.

? Bury lots of plastic letters. Now find the letters of your name, other words, or all the letters of the alphabet.

? Bury plastic numbers, then challenge your friend to find the answer to simple calculations - eg 'Can you find the answer to 3+5?'

? Put 'buried treasure' in Google web and try some of the activities you find there.

? If you put sequins or small beads in sand, how can you get them out again? Experiment with different tools and methods. Draw pictures of your findings.

? Find six small objects. Draw each one on paper or card. Hide the objects and shuffle the pictures. lay the pictures in a sequence and see if you can find the objects in the right order. Now challenge some friends.

? Make a mixture of dry sand, sequins, lentils, beans, beads and seeds. Use a timer or the clock to time how long it takes to sort all the things out again.

Ready for more?

- Make a secret message in plastic letters. Bury your message and mix up the letters. Now challenge a friend to find the message.

- Make a treasure map and bury objects at special places shown on the map.

- Bury the pieces of a jigsaw in DRY sand. Can you make the jigsaw by finding all the hidden pieces?

- Bury some old objects. Can you put them on a time line in chronological order when you have found them all?

- Find and hide some objects, then make up a story using each object as you find it. Put the objects in a row so you can remember your story. Now bury them again and make up a new story.

- Choose a pebble each. Look carefully at your own pebble and draw it. Bury all the pebbles and see if you can match them up with the drawings as you find each one.

- A game for two to four people. Find a scarf or blindfold (a soft fabric head band works well). Now bury some objects in the sand and take turns to wear the blindfold as you find an object and name it just by touch. If you are right, keep the object, if not, bury it again. The player with the most objects at the end of the game is the winner.

Materials, equipment suppliers, websites, books and other references

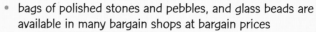

Suppliers and sources:

You can bury anything, here are some ideas:

- foreign and out of circulation coins or plastic medals
- bags of polished stones and pebbles, and glass beads are available in many bargain shops at bargain prices
- shells and stones of unusual shapes
- make a Christmas collection of the objects from crackers
- many bargain shops have cheap bags of small animals, insects, dinosaurs etc
- get beads and other jewels from charity shops and markets
- jigsaws (preferably wooden ones that don't get damp in the sand)
- sequins are cheap and come in all sorts of shapes and sizes

www.philipandtacey.co.uk have a dazzling collection of sequins, beads, glass beads and other objects to hide in or mix with sand. You could even buy some of their bags of googly eyes to bury and find! They also have plastic letters and numbers.

www.outlandstone.co.uk sell stones and pebbles in lovely colours, look at the pictures, but you have to buy at least 25kg of each or share a bag!

www.emporiumuk.biz have a massive range of glass beads, marbles and other decorative beads.

Use Google Images for pictures - some suggestions for words to search: 'treasure', 'treasure island', 'treasure map', 'pirate', 'pirate ship', 'gold', 'jewels', 'necklace', 'beads'.

Some books:

Treasure Island (Junior Classics); Robert Louis Stevenson; Naxos Audio Books (CD)
Pirate Pete; Kim Kennedy; Harry N Abrahams
Noelle's Treasure Tale - book and CD; Gloria Estefan; Rayo
Pam's Maps; Pippe Goodhart; Red Fox

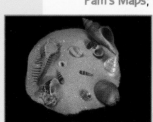

Felix and the Blue Dragon; Angela McAllister; Orion Children's
Berenstain Bears Seashore Treasure; Stan Berenstain; Harper Collins
Dolphin Treasure; Wayne Grover; Harper Trophy
Duncan Cameron's Shipwreck Detective; Richard Platt; DK Publishing.

Curriculum coverage grid overleaf

Full version of KS1 PoS on pages 69-74
Photopcopiable version on page 8

Literacy

Lit 1 speak	Lit 2 listen	Lit 3 group	Lit 4 drama	Lit 5 word	Lit 6 spell	Lit 7 text1	Lit 8 text2	Lit 9 text3	Lit10 text4	Lit11 sentence	Lit12 presentation
1.1	2.1	3.1	4.1	5.1	6.1	7.1	8.1	9.1	10.1	11.1	12.1
1.2	2.2	3.2	4.2	5.2	6.2	7.2	8.2	9.2	10.2	11.2	12.2

Numeracy

Num 1 U&A	Num 2 count	Num 3 number	Num 4 calculate	Num 5 shape	Num 6 measure	Num 7 data
1.1	2.1	3.1	4.1	5.1	6.1	7.1
1.2	2.2	3.2	4.2	5.2	6.2	7.2

Science

SC1 Enquiry			SC2 Life processes					SC3 Materials		SC4 Phys processes		
Sc1.1	Sc1.2	Sc1.3	Sc2.1	Sc2.2	Sc2.3	Sc2.4	Sc2.5	Sc3.1	Sc3.2	Sc4.1	Sc4.2	Sc4.3
1.1a	1.2a	1.3a	2.1a	2.2a	2.3a	2.4a	2.5a	3.1a	3.2a	4.1a	4.2a	4.3a
1.1b	1.2b	1.3b	2.1b	2.2b	2.3b	2.4b	2.5b	3.1b	3.2b	4.1b	4.2b	4.3b
1.1c	1.2c	1.3c	2.1c	2.2c	2.3c		2.5c	3.1c		4.1c	4.2c	4.3c
1.1d				2.2d				3.1d				4.3d
				2.2e								
				2.2f								
				2.2g								

ICT

ICT 1 finding out		ICT 2 ideas	ICT 3 reviewing	ICT 4 breadth
1.1a	1.2a	2a	3a	4a
1.1b	1.2b	2b	3b	4b
1.1c	1.2c	2c	3c	4c
	1.2d			

D&T

D&T 1 developing	D&T 2 tool use	D&T 3 evaluating	D&T 4 materials	D&T 5 breadth
1a	2a	3a	4a	5a
1b	2b	3b	4b	5b
1c	2c			5c
1d	2d			
1e	2e			

History

H1 chronology	H2 events, people	H3 interpret	H4 enquire	H5 org & comm	H6 breadth
1a	2a	3a	4a	5a	6a
1b	2b		4b		6b
					6c
					6d

Geography

G1.1 & G1.2 enquiry		G2 places	G3 processes	G4 environment	G5 breadth
1.1a	1.2a	2a	3a	4a	5a
1.1b	1.2b	2b	3b	4b	5b
1.1c	1.2c	2c			5c
1.1d	1.2d	2d			5d
		2e			

Music

M1 performing	M2 composing	M3 appraising	M4 listening	M5 breadth
1a	2a	3a	4a	5a
1b	2b	3b	4b	5b
1c			4c	5c
				5d

PHSE & C

PSHEC1 conf & resp	PSHEC2 citizenship	PSHEC3 health	PSHEC4 relationships
1a	2a	3a	4a
1b	2b	3b	4b
1c	2c	3c	4c
1d	2d	3d	4d
1e	2e	3e	4e
	2f	3f	
	2g	3g	
	2h		

Art & Design

A&D1 ideas	A&D2 making	A&D3 evaluating	A&D4 materials	A&D5 breadth
1a	2a	3a	4a	5a
1b	2b	3b	4b	5b
	2c		4c	5c
				5d

PE

PE1 devel skills	PE2 apply skills	PE3 evaluate	PE4 fitness	PE5 breadth
1a	2a	3a	4a	5a dance
1b	2b	3b	4b	5b games
	2c	3c		5c gym

Critical skills	Thinking Skills
problem solving	observing
decision making	classifying
critical thinking	prediction
creative thinking	making inferences
communication	problem solving
organisation	drawing conclusions
management	
leadership	

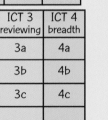

Imagined worlds

Imagined worlds

Previous experience in the Foundation Stage

Making environments for small world and other fantasy situations will be familiar to children. In the Foundation Stage they may have had experience of these materials:

* in free play indoors and out of doors;
* combined with small world people and animals, vehicles etc;
* combined with malleable materials such as clay or dough;
* for story telling;
* for exploring sequence, character and plot;
* in sand, water, malleable materials, clay, gravel, compost, mud.

Pause for thought

In the early stages of working with these materials it is crucial to continue to observe the children. Only by doing this can you set developmentally appropriate challenges and provocations. The ideas listed here are offered as suggestions; the most exciting challenges will arise from children's own interests and motivations, which will only become apparent as you spend time with them, watching and joining them in their play. As you do this, you will be moving between the three interconnecting roles of observer, co-player, extender described below, and will be able to decide what you need to do next to take the learning forward.

The responsive adult (see page 5)

In three interconnecting roles, the responsive adult will be:

observer

* observing
* listening
* interpreting

co-player

* **modelling**
* **playing alongside**
* **offering suggestions**
* **responding sensitively**
* **initiating with care!**

extender

* discussing ideas
* sharing thinking
* modelling new skills
* asking open questions
* being an informed extender
* instigating ideas & thoughts
* supporting children as they make links in learning
* making possibilities evident
* introducing new ideas and resources
* offering challenges and provocations

Offering challenges and provocations - some ideas:

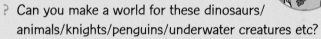

Children will probably have had free experience of these activities and materials, and may not be used to adult initiation or direction through specific challenges. You may have to go slowly and be patient if their focus strays and they play something completely different!

? Can you make a world for these dinosaurs/ animals/knights/penguins/underwater creatures etc?

? Collect some twigs, leaves and other natural materials from home or the school garden and make an imagined forest or mountainside.

? Put some plastic animals and reptiles in a bag. Now take just one handful of creatures and make an environment for them.

? Put some word cards in the bag - 'jungle' 'desert' 'space' 'mountain' 'seaside'. Pull out one card and make the world it says.

? Using a flat builders' tray and some foil, make a space landscape. Add some spacemen or space monsters made from clay or plasticene.

? Draw a fantasy landscape for superheroes. Using the sand as a base, build some structures such as buildings, bridges and tunnels for the superheroes to move in. Now make up a superhero story with your friends, using the landscape.

? Make a sand tray world for your favourite story character. Add creatures, trees and plants, buildings or people. Take some photos of your landscape and make a new story book with your photos.

? Use sand and water to make a fantasy island. Add other objects and things you find to make your island as exciting and interesting as possible. Now use some animals or people to make up an island story. Tell your story to someone else when you have decided what it is.

Ready for more?

- Work with some friends to design and make a fantasy landscape. Decide who will do the drawing, the research, the building, take the photos, do a commentary. Make sure you take photos right from the start of your project, and keep taking them throughout and at the end. Make a Power Point presentation of your project.

- Look on Google for some pictures of film and TV characters. Print off some pictures and stick them on card to make characters. Now make a scene for your character to inhabit.

- Be a film designer. Watch 'Finding Nemo', 'Jungle Book', 'Star Wars', 'Planet Earth' or another video and make some sets for the characters in the film. Draw the characters and stick on card or make them from plasticene. Or you could use the small toy versions of the film characters.

- Pick a story book and look carefully at one of the pictures. Can you make a replica with sand and other objects? Try to make the model as accurate as possible.

- How can you make a model volcano with the sand? Look for some pictures on Google images and have a go. What could you use to make molten lava flows, and fire at the top of your volcano? Can you make the sand flow down the sides of your volcano? Make up an adventure story about this dangerous place.

Materials, equipment suppliers, websites, books and other references

Resources:

You will have many objects and materials for starting imagined world play in trays or small boxes of sand. These include:

- dinosaurs and farm/zoo animals
- fantasy characters, including the small versions of superhero toys
- Playmobil, Lego and other characters from construction sets
- comics, catalogues and magazines with pictures for the children to cut out and mount on card
- clay, dough and plasticene for characters and models
- add sawn logs, collect twigs and leaves, dig up some stones and pebbles

Film and TV characters are often good story starters for imagined world, ask the children to bring in favourites. And of course, any story you tell can be the start of a new activity for the children, making or finding their own character figures and making their own environments.

Look at www.philipandtacey.co.uk for Active World Mats - which are Builders' trays with sets of characters for small world imaginative play. TTS group www.tts-group.co.uk also stock these.

Google images: 'disney', or enter the name of a character such as 'bambi' 'nemo' 'superman' 'princess' 'cinderella' 'lion king' 'volcano' etc.

and **Google web search** for 'disney', 'family.go.com', or animal or character names. You could also try some of the sites for teachers (in the UK and abroad) for activities and templates for making characters - here are a few:

www.activitiesforkids.com and www.thekidzpage.com have free clip art www.bbc.co.uk has sections for schools and parents with activities and printable sheets.

Books and Publications:

There are so many suitable stories that we are not suggesting titles, but you could explore books on fantasy landscapes for older children, or titles on architectural models or theatre design.

Curriculum coverage grid overleaf

Literacy

Lit 1 speak	Lit 2 listen	Lit 3 group	Lit 4 drama	Lit 5 word	Lit 6 spell	Lit 7 text1	Lit 8 text2	Lit 9 text3	Lit10 text4	Lit11 sentence	Lit12 presentation
1.1	2.1	3.1	4.1	5.1	6.1	7.1	8.1	9.1	10.1	11.1	12.1
1.2	2.2	3.2	4.2	5.2	6.2	7.2	8.2	9.2	10.2	11.2	12.2

Numeracy

Num 1 U&A	Num 2 count	Num 3 number	Num 4 calculate	Num 5 shape	Num 6 measure	Num 7 data
1.1	2.1	3.1	4.1	5.1	6.1	7.1
1.2	2.2	3.2	4.2	5.2	6.2	7.2

Science

SC1 Enquiry			SC2 Life processes					SC3 Materials		SC4 Phys processes		
Sc1.1	Sc1.2	Sc1.3	Sc2.1	Sc2.2	Sc2.3	Sc2.4	Sc2.5	Sc3.1	Sc3.2	Sc4.1	Sc4.2	Sc4.3
1.1a	1.2a	1.3a	2.1a	2.2a	2.3a	2.4a	2.5a	3.1a	3.2a	4.1a	4.2a	4.3a
1.1b	1.2b	1.3b	2.1b	2.2b	2.3b	2.4b	2.5b	3.1b	3.2b	4.1b	4.2b	4.3b
1.1c	1.2c	1.3c	2.1c	2.2c	2.3c		2.5c	3.1c		4.1c	4.2c	4.3c
1.1d				2.2d				3.1d				4.3d
				2.2e								
				2.2f								
				2.2g								

ICT

ICT 1 finding out		ICT 2 ideas	ICT 3 reviewing	ICT 4 breadth
1.1a	1.2a	2a	3a	4a
1.1b	1.2b	2b	3b	4b
1.1c	1.2c	2c	3c	4c
	1.2d			

Full version of KS1 PoS on pages 69-74
Photopcopiable version on page 8

D&T

D&T 1 developing	D&T 2 tool use	D&T 3 evaluating	D&T 4 materials	D&T 5 breadth
1a	2a	3a	4a	5a
1b	2b	3b	4b	5b
1c	2c			5c
1d	2d			
1e	2e			

History

H1 chronology	H2 events, people	H3 interpret	H4 enquire	H5 org & comm	H6 breadth
1a	2a	3a	4a	5a	6a
1b	2b		4b		6b
					6c
					6d

Geography

G1.1 & G1.2 enquiry		G2 places	G3 processes	G4 environment	G5 breadth
1.1a	1.2a	2a	3a	4a	5a
1.1b	1.2b	2b	3b	4b	5b
1.1c	1.2c	2c			5c
1.1d	1.2d	2d			5d
		2e			

Music

M1 performing	M2 composing	M3 appraising	M4 listening	M5 breadth
1a	2a	3a	4a	5a
1b	2b	3b	4b	5b
1c			4c	5c
				5d

PHSE & C

PSHEC1 conf & resp	PSHEC2 citizenship	PSHEC3 health	PSHEC4 relationships
1a	2a	3a	4a
1b	2b	3b	4b
1c	2c	3c	4c
1d	2d	3d	4d
1e	2e	3e	4e
	2f	3f	
	2g	3g	
	2h		

Art & Design

A&D1 ideas	A&D2 making	A&D3 evaluating	A&D4 materials	A&D5 breadth
1a	2a	3a	4a	5a
1b	2b	3b	4b	5b
	2c		4c	5c
				5d

PE

PE1 devel skills	PE2 apply skills	PE3 evaluate	PE4 fitness	PE5 breadth
1a	2a	3a	4a	5a dance
1b	2b	3b	4b	5b games
	2c	3c		5c gym

Photo copyright ASCO

Critical skills	Thinking Skills
problem solving	observing
decision making	classifying
critical thinking	prediction
creative thinking	making inferences
communication	problem solving
organisation	drawing conclusions
management	
leadership	

Caves and tunnels

Caves and tunnels

Previous experience in the Foundation Stage

During their time in the Foundation Stage children will have experimented with making tunnels and caves in various ways during:

* free play indoors and outside, in sand and mud;
* in wet sand;
* by exploring the holes made by insects and small animals;

They will have made caves and tunnels when:

* making dens with boxes and drapes;
* playing with construction, small world toys and train tracks;
* playing on large apparatus.

They may also have experienced being in tunnels in cars and trains, and some may have been through the Channel Tunnel or visited caves.

Pause for thought

In the early stages of working with these materials it is crucial to continue to observe the children. Only by doing this can you set developmentally appropriate challenges and provocations. The ideas listed here are offered as suggestions; the most exciting challenges will arise from children's own interests and motivations, which will only become apparent as you spend time with them, watching and joining them in their play. As you do this, you will be moving between the three interconnecting roles of observer, co-player, extender described below, and will be able to decide what you need to do next to take the learning forward.

The responsive adult (see page 5)

In three interconnecting roles, the responsive adult will be:

* observing
* listening
* interpreting

observer

* **modelling**
* **playing alongside**
* **offering suggestions**
* **responding sensitively**
* **initiating with care!**

co-player

* discussing ideas
* sharing thinking
* modelling new skills
* asking open questions
* being an informed extender
* instigating ideas & thoughts
* supporting children as they make links in learning
* making possibilities evident
* introducing new ideas and resources
* offering challenges and provocations

extender

Offering challenges and provocations - some ideas:

? Can you make a tunnel in the sand that a car can travel through?
? Can you make a tunnel that is strong enough for a car to go over the top?
? Who can make the widest, or the longest tunnel?
? Can you make a tunnel that turns a corner or goes round an obstacle?
? Can you work with a partner to make a tunnel, starting at opposite ends and meeting in the middle? Put 'Channel Tunnel' in Google to find out how they did it!
? Make a tunnel that Action man or Barbie can get through.
? Make a cave for a family of dinosaurs.
? Make a cave for a soft toy or a some small world animals that live in caves.
? Can you make a cave for some cave men? It needs a good lookout place, and to be safe from dangerous animals.
? Look in the library for some books about caves and tunnels. Take some photos of your caves and tunnels and make a display in your classroom.
? Some tunnels need strengthening or they collapse. How could you make your tunnels stronger?
? Make up a story about getting trapped in a tunnel, and tell the story by making the tunnel and using small world characters.
? Find a train track set (you may have to borrow one from another class). Now set the train track up in the sand tray and experiment with making tunnels for the trains to go through. You may need to use supports for your tunnels to make them longer and stronger.

Ready for more?

- Draw a plan for a series of tunnels that connect with each other.  Make the tunnels to match your plan. What are the difficulties with making tunnels? How can you overcome these?

- Make a building from Lego or boxes. Now put it in the sand and make a secret cave underneath the building. How can you support the building?

- Explore different ways of supporting and reinforcing tunnels and caves. What works best? Take some photos of your ideas.

- Plan and make a series of caves linked by tunnels. Add some play people and make up some adventure stories. If you take photos, you could make a story book for your friends to read.

- How can you use mirrors to look inside your tunnels and caves? Can you take a photo of the inside of a cave or tunnel? Can you make features on the roofs of the caves and tunnels?

- Find some pictures of cave animals. Try this site www.kathimitchell.com and click on 'caves' for some great ideas for making cave habitats. Look in your library for cave dwelling animals to live in the caves you have made.

- Use some thin fabric to dress some small world people as cave people and make a habitat for them with a cave, lookout and hunting area with animals.

Materials, equipment suppliers, websites, books and other references

Some ideas for **resources and equipment**:
Collect materials for supporting and propping the sand - these could include:

- fallen sticks, collected on walks to the woods
- masking tape and duct tape from bargain and 'Pound' shops
- offcuts of plywood or pieces of driftwood
- card and plastic tubing, plastic bottles with the tops and bottoms cut off, plastic bowls and boxes
- plastic netting, plaster bandage (such as Modroc)

The very best site about caves for teachers and children is www.kathimitchell.com click on 'caves' in the science section on the right of the page - it has lots of links to other sites about caves, cave animals, make your own stalactites, cave terms, photos, screen savers etc - you could spend a whole term here, using the links and information.
Other sites include:

http.arachnophiliac.co.uk - for spiders, snakes and other animals that live underground.
www.wookey.co.uk the site for Wookey Hole Caves, with photos.
www.cheddarcaves.co.uk and www.whitescarcave.co.uk which has a good virtual tour of the caves. www.caving.uk.com is a site for cavers.

Google images: 'cave', 'caving', 'tunnel', 'forest den', 'burrow', 'stalactite'.

Books and Other Publications:
I wonder why Stalactites Hang Down; Jackie Gaff; Kingfisher
I wonder why Tunnels are Round; Steve Parker; Kingfisher
Crypts, Caves and Tunnels of London; Ian Marchant; Watling Street Ltd

Cave animals (animals and their habitats); Francine Galko; Heinemann
Caves; Jeanne Hanson; Chelsea House
The Dak-Dak series - the hidden caves of Oslama; Susan Van de Leucht; Lulu.com
The Channel Tunnel; S Donvan; Lerner Publishing

Curriculum coverage grid overleaf

Full version of KS1 PoS on pages 69-74
Photopcopiable version on page 8

Literacy

	Lit 1 speak	Lit 2 listen	Lit 3 group	Lit 4 drama	Lit 5 word	Lit 6 spell	Lit 7 text1	Lit 8 text2	Lit 9 text3	Lit10 text4	Lit11 sentence	Lit12 presentation
	1.1	2.1	3.1	4.1	5.1	6.1	7.1	8.1	9.1	10.1	11.1	12.1
	1.2	2.2	3.2	4.2	5.2	6.2	7.2	8.2	9.2	10.2	11.2	12.2

Numeracy

	Num 1 U&A	Num 2 count	Num 3 number	Num 4 calculate	Num 5 shape	Num 6 measure	Num 7 data
	1.1	2.1	3.1	4.1	5.1	6.1	7.1
	1.2	2.2	3.2	4.2	5.2	6.2	7.2

Science

SC1 Enquiry			SC2 Life processes					SC3 Materials		SC4 Phys processes		
Sc1.1	Sc1.2	Sc1.3	Sc2.1	Sc2.2	Sc2.3	Sc2.4	Sc2.5	Sc3.1	Sc3.2	Sc4.1	Sc4.2	Sc4.3
1.1a	1.2a	1.3a	2.1a	2.2a	2.3a	2.4a	2.5a	3.1a	3.2a	4.1a	4.2a	4.3a
1.1b	1.2b	1.3b	2.1b	2.2b	2.3b	2.4b	2.5b	3.1b	3.2b	4.1b	4.2b	4.3b
1.1c	1.2c	1.3c	2.1c	2.2c	2.3c		2.5c	3.1c		4.1c	4.2c	4.3c
1.1d				2.2d				3.1d				4.3d
				2.2e								
				2.2f								
				2.2g								

ICT

ICT 1 finding out		ICT 2 ideas	ICT 3 reviewing	ICT 4 breadth
1.1a	1.2a	2a	3a	4a
1.1b	1.2b	2b	3b	4b
1.1c	1.2c	2c	3c	4c
	1.2d			

D&T

D&T 1 developing	D&T 2 tool use	D&T 3 evaluating	D&T 4 materials	D&T 5 breadth
1a	2a	3a	4a	5a
1b	2b	3b	4b	5b
1c	2c			5c
1d	2d			
1e	2e			

History

H1 chronology	H2 events, people	H3 interpret	H4 enquire	H5 org & comm	H6 breadth
1a	2a	3a	4a	5a	6a
1b	2b		4b		6b
					6c
					6d

Geography

G1.1 & G1.2 enquiry		G2 places	G3 processes	G4 environment	G5 breadth
1.1a	1.2a	2a	3a	4a	5a
1.1b	1.2b	2b	3b	4b	5b
1.1c	1.2c	2c			5c
1.1d	1.2d	2d			5d
		2e			

Music

M1 performing	M2 composing	M3 appraising	M4 listening	M5 breadth
1a	2a	3a	4a	5a
1b	2b	3b	4b	5b
1c			4c	5c
				5d

PHSE & C

PSHEC1 conf & resp	PSHEC2 citizenship	PSHEC3 health	PSHEC4 relationships
1a	2a	3a	4a
1b	2b	3b	4b
1c	2c	3c	4c
1d	2d	3d	4d
1e	2e	3e	4e
	2f	3f	
	2g	3g	
	2h		

Art & Design

A&D1 ideas	A&D2 making	A&D3 evaluating	A&D4 materials	A&D5 breadth
1a	2a	3a	4a	5a
1b	2b	3b	4b	5b
	2c		4c	5c
				5d

PE

PE1 devel skills	PE2 apply skills	PE3 evaluate	PE4 fitness	PE5 breadth
1a	2a	3a	4a	5a dance
1b	2b	3b	4b	5b games
	2c	3c		5c gym

Critical skills	Thinking Skills
problem solving	observing
decision making	classifying
critical thinking	prediction
creative thinking	making inferences
communication	problem solving
organisation	drawing conclusions
management	
leadership	

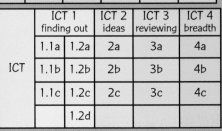

Story book creations

Story book creations

Previous experience in the Foundation Stage.

Children will probably have had experience of working with story book characters in sand, especially those from traditional stories such as The Gingerbread Man, Little Red Riding Hood etc. These may have been in:

* free play both indoors and outside;
* dressing up as story book characters;
* using puppets to represent story characters;
* using small world figures to develop story scenes or a narrative;
* a wide range of traditional stories and picture books by significant authors;
* working with wet and dry sand and gravel to explore its properties;
* using sand to create a range of habitats.

Pause for thought

In the early stages of working with these materials it is crucial to continue to observe the children. Only by doing this can you set developmentally appropriate challenges and provocations. The ideas listed here are offered as suggestions; the most exciting challenges will arise from children's own interests and motivations, which will only become apparent as you spend time with them, watching and joining them in their play. As you do this, you will be moving between the three interconnecting roles of observer, co-player, extender described below, and will be able to decide what you need to do next to take the learning forward.

The responsive adult (see page 5)

In three interconnecting roles, the responsive adult will be:

* observing
* listening
* interpreting

observer

* **modelling**
* **playing alongside**
* **offering suggestions**
* **responding sensitively**
* **initiating with care!**

co-player

* discussing ideas
* sharing thinking
* modelling new skills
* asking open questions
* being an informed extender
* instigating ideas & thoughts
* supporting children as they make links in learning
* making possibilities evident
* introducing new ideas and resources
* offering challenges and provocations

extender

Offering Challenges and Provocations - some ideas:

? Can you make a scene in the sand that could be used for the cover of a book you know?

? Can you make a scene that could be used as an advert or poster for one of your favourite books?

? Could you produce a series of scenes that would tell a story? This could either be one you already know or one you make up.

? Make an alternative ending to a story you know.

? Could you make a setting and use story book characters to help you tell a story to other children?

? Use plasticene, clay or dough to make some characters of your own. Use a digital camera to make a story with your characters.

? Collect some card, wood, twigs, string, stones, branches, foil, pebbles, shells and other objects to add to the sand to make your scenes and stories more interesting, exciting and varied.

? Use damp sand to make caves, towers, castles or cottages for your characters and stories. Find ways to support your structures, and spray them with water to keep the sand damp.

? Choose a story book and look closely at the pictures. Make a replica of one of the pictures using sand, gravel, pebbles, and other natural objects to help to make it realistic. Take some photos and make a display with your scene, characters and the story book.

? Get some branches and use them to make a cave for a story. Use some story characters to make up an exciting cave story. You could use fabric and card to turn Lego or Playmobil people into characters - a horse into a unicorn, a man into a king, a woman into a witch!

Ready for more?

- ✏ Use a big sand tray to make a story map - eg Red Riding Hood's house, the woods, the path to Grandmother's house etc, or Rosie's Walk or The Bear Hunt.

- ✏ Can you produce and photograph 12 different story settings for a calendar?

- ✏ Could you produce a 'Guess the Story' book by producing a range of scenes and taking photos.

- ✏ Make a new story from an old one - eg We're Going on a Dinosaur Hunt; The Three Tigers; Super Rabbit; The Magic Stone.

- ✏ Make a story plan or a story board on paper, then make the scenes and characters for your own original story.

- ✏ Make settings for Doctor Who, films, Superman, favourite pop groups.

- ✏ Work as a class to make all the different scenes for a longer story such as The Iron Man or The Hobbit. You can make clothes for characters from thin fabric, and props from card or plastic. Make some backgrounds for your story by drawing or painting the scenes on pieces of card and bending or scoring them so they can stand up at the back of the sand tray. Add stones for rocks, boxes for buildings, twigs for trees, piles of sand for mountains. Take photos as you tell the story, so you can make a display.

Materials, equipment suppliers, websites, books and other references

Some ideas for resources and equipment:

Recycled materials are free, so make sure the children have plenty of choice and can get the things they want to use as they work with sand and gravel.

Put a notice up inviting offers of CLEAN recycled materials such as:

- • small cardboard tubes and boxes and cones, egg boxes
- • plastic bottles and tops, containers, cups, tubs and pots
- • plastic and polystyrene trays, bubble wrap
- • offcuts of paper and wallpaper, newspapers, junk mail and magazines
- • plastic and paper carriers, paper bags
- • string, wool, pipe cleaners, soft wire, cord and rope; sticks, twigs, small logs
- • scraps of fabric to make clothes for home made characters

Leave a box by the notice, so parents and children can drop their offerings in. Then you can sort and check them for suitability, Health and Safety and cleanliness.

It's important to give children plenty of time to work on their projects and to find some way of protecting unfinished projects, particularly if you are expecting them to photograph the story for a book or presentation.

TTS group www.tts-group.co.uk and Early Learning Centre have tough digital and video cameras that are easy for children to use.

Google images: try putting characters or scenes such as 'forest' 'farm' 'castle' 'island' 'tower' for images to inspire their work.

Traditional story characters, scenes and other story telling resources from Yellow Door www.yellow-door.net

Books and Publications:

Collect a good range of picture books with illustrations that can inspire children's work. Discuss the story and the pictures as you encourage children to experiment with making scenes and enacting the stories. Encourage them to bring or make characters to inhabit the story landscapes they make.

Curriculum coverage grid overleap

Potential NC KS1 Curriculum Coverage through the provocations suggested for Story books

Full version of KS1 PoS on pages 69-74
Photopcopiable version on page 8

Literacy

	Lit 1 speak	Lit 2 listen	Lit 3 group	Lit 4 drama	Lit 5 word	Lit 6 spell	Lit 7 text1	Lit 8 text2	Lit 9 text3	Lit10 text4	Lit11 sentence	Lit12 presentation
	1.1	2.1	3.1	4.1	5.1	6.1	7.1	8.1	9.1	10.1	11.1	12.1
	1.2	2.2	3.2	4.2	5.2	6.2	7.2	8.2	9.2	10.2	11.2	12.2

Numeracy

	Num 1 U&A	Num 2 count	Num 3 number	Num 4 calculate	Num 5 shape	Num 6 measure	Num 7 data
	1.1	2.1	3.1	4.1	5.1	6.1	7.1
	1.2	2.2	3.2	4.2	5.2	6.2	7.2

Science

	SC1 Enquiry			SC2 Life processes					SC3 Materials		SC4 Phys processes		
	Sc1.1	Sc1.2	Sc1.3	Sc2.1	Sc2.2	Sc2.3	Sc2.4	Sc2.5	Sc3.1	Sc3.2	Sc4.1	Sc4.2	Sc4.3
	1.1a	1.2a	1.3a	2.1a	2.2a	2.3a	2.4a	2.5a	3.1a	3.2a	4.1a	4.2a	4.3a
	1.1b	1.2b	1.3b	2.1b	2.2b	2.3b	2.4b	2.5b	3.1b	3.2b	4.1b	4.2b	4.3b
	1.1c	1.2c	1.3c	2.1c	2.2c	2.3c		2.5c	3.1c		4.1c	4.2c	4.3c
	1.1d				2.2d				3.1d				4.3d
					2.2e								
					2.2f								
					2.2g								

ICT

	ICT 1 finding out		ICT 2 ideas	ICT 3 reviewing	ICT 4 breadth
	1.1a	1.2a	2a	3a	4a
	1.1b	1.2b	2b	3b	4b
	1.1c	1.2c	2c	3c	4c
		1.2d			

D&T

	D&T 1 developing	D&T 2 tool use	D&T 3 evaluating	D&T 4 materials	D&T 5 breadth
	1a	2a	3a	4a	5a
	1b	2b	3b	4b	5b
	1c	2c			5c
	1d	2d			
	1e	2e			

History

	H1 chronology	H2 events, people	H3 interpret	H4 enquire	H5 org & comm	H6 breadth
	1a	2a	3a	4a	5a	6a
	1b	2b		4b		6b
						6c
						6d

Geography

	G1.1 & G1.2 enquiry		G2 places	G3 processes	G4 environment	G5 breadth
	1.1a	1.2a	2a	3a	4a	5a
	1.1b	1.2b	2b	3b	4b	5b
	1.1c	1.2c	2c			5c
	1.1d	1.2d	2d			5d
			2e			

Music

	M1 performing	M2 composing	M3 appraising	M4 listening	M5 breadth
	1a	2a	3a	4a	5a
	1b	2b	3b	4b	5b
	1c			4c	5c
					5d

PHSE & C

	PSHEC1 conf & resp	PSHEC2 citizenship	PSHEC3 health	PSHEC4 relationships
	1a	2a	3a	4a
	1b	2b	3b	4b
	1c	2c	3c	4c
	1d	2d	3d	4d
	1e	2e	3e	4e
		2f	3f	
		2g	3g	
		2h		

Art & Design

	A&D1 ideas	A&D2 making	A&D3 evaluating	A&D4 materials	A&D5 breadth
	1a	2a	3a	4a	5a
	1b	2b	3b	4b	5b
		2c		4c	5c
					5d

PE

	PE1 devel skills	PE2 apply skills	PE3 evaluate	PE4 fitness	PE5 breadth
	1a	2a	3a	4a	5a dance
	1b	2b	3b	4b	5b games
		2c	3c		5c gym

Critical skills	Thinking Skills
problem solving	observing
decision making	classifying
critical thinking	prediction
creative thinking	making inferences
communication	problem solving
organisation	drawing conclusions
management	
leadership	

Materials from Yellow Door

The following pages contain the detail for the curriculum key which appears at the end of each section of the book. The appendix consists of the following:

1. Short-hand versions of the QCA/DfES Programme of Study for Key Stage 1 in:

> Science
> Information & Communication Technology
> Design and Technology
> History
> Geography
> Music
> Art and Design
> Physical Education

2. The suggested programme of study for Personal, Social and Health Education and Citizenship (PSHE & C)

3. The elements of the guidance for learning and teaching of Literacy and Numeracy in Years 1 and 2 (from the Primary Framework for literacy and mathematics; DfES/SureStart; Sept 2006; Ref: 02011-2006BOK-EN)

Literacy 1 speaking	Literacy 2 listening & responding	Literacy 3 group discussion & interaction	Literacy 4 drama	Literacy 5 word recognition, coding & decoding	Literacy 6 word structure & spelling	Literacy 7 understanding & interpreting texts	Literacy 8 engaging & responding to text	Literacy 9 creating and shaping texts	Literacy 10 text structure & organisation	Literacy 11 sentence structure & punctuation	Literacy 12 presentation
Year 1 Tell stories and describe incidents from their own experience in an audible voice Retell stories, ordering events using story language Interpret a text by reading aloud with some variety in pace and emphasis **Experiment with & build new stores of words** to communicate in different contexts	**Year 1** Listen with sustained concentration, building new stores of words in different contexts **Listen to and follow instructions** accurately, asking for help and clarification if necessary Listen to tapes or video and express views about how a story or information has been presented	**Year 1** Take turns to speak, listen to others' suggestions and talk about what they are going to do Ask and answer questions, make relevant contributions, offer suggestions and take turns **Explain their views to others** in a small group, decide how to report the group's views to the class	**Year 1** Explore familiar themes and characters through improvisation and role-play **Act out their own and well-known stories**, using voices for characters Discuss why they like a performance	**Year 1** Recognise and use alternative ways of pronouncing the graphemes already taught, for example, that the grapheme 'g' is pronounced differently in 'get' and 'gem'; the grapheme 'ow' is pronounced differently in 'how' and 'show' Recognise and use alternative ways of spelling the phonemes already taught, for example 'ae' ' can be spelt with 'ai', 'ay' or 'a-e'; begin to know which words contain which spelling alternatives **Identify the constituent parts of two-syllable and three-syllable words** to support the application of phonic knowledge and skills Recognise automatically an increasing number of familiar high frequency words Apply phonic knowledge and skills as the prime approach to reading and spelling unfamiliar words that are not completely decodable **Read more challenging texts** which can be decoded using their acquired phonic knowledge and skills; automatic recognition of high frequency words Read and spell phonically decodable two-syllable and three-syllable words	**Year 1** Spell new words using phonics as the prime approach Segment sounds into their constituent phonemes in order to spell them correctly Children **move from spelling simple CVC words to longer words** that include common diagraphs and adjacent consonants such as 'brush', 'crunch' **Recognise and use alternative ways of spelling the graphemes already taught**, for example that the /ae/ sound can be spelt with 'ai', 'ay' or 'a-e'; that the /ee/ sound can also be spelt as 'ea' and 'e'; & begin to know which words contain which spelling alternatives Use knowledge of common inflections in spelling, such as plurals, -ly, -er **Read and spell phonically decodable 2- & 3 syllable words**	**Year 1** **Identify the main events and characters in stories**, and find specific information in simple texts Use syntax and context when reading for meaning **Make predictions** showing an understanding of ideas, events and characters Recognise the main elements that shape different texts **Explore the effect of patterns of language** and repeated words and phrases	**Year 1** Select books for personal reading and give reasons for choices **Visualise and comment on events, characters and ideas,** making imaginative links to their own experiences Distinguish fiction and non-fiction texts and the different purposes for reading them	**Year 1** Independently **choose what to write about**, plan and follow it through Use key features **of narrative in their own writing** Convey information and ideas in simple non-narrative forms **Find and use new and interesting words and phrases**, including story language **Create short simple texts on paper and on screen** that combine words with images (and sounds)	**Year 1** Write chronological and non-chronological texts using simple structures **Group written sentences together in chunks** of meaning or subject	**Year 1** Compose and write simple sentences independently to communicate meaning Use capital letters and full stops when punctuating simple sentences	**Year 1** Write most letters, correctly formed and orientated, using a comfortable and efficient pencil grip **Write with spaces between words** accurately Use the space bar and keyboard to type their name and simple texts
Year 2 Speak with clarity and use appropriate intonation when reading and reciting texts **Tell real and imagined stories** using the conventions of familiar story language Explain ideas and processes using imaginative and adventurous vocabulary and non-verbal gestures to support communication	**Year 2** Listen to others in class, ask relevant questions and follow instructions Listen to talk by an adult, remember some specific points and identify what they have learned **Respond to presentations** by describing characters, repeating some highlight and commenting constructively	**Year 2** Ensure that everyone contributes, allocate tasks, and consider alternatives and reach agreement **Work effectively in groups** by ensuring that each group member takes a turn challenging, supporting and moving on Listen to each other's views and preferences, agree the next steps to take and identify contributions by each group member	**Year 2** Adopt appropriate roles in small or large groups and consider alternative courses of action Present part of traditional stories, their own stories or work drawn from different parts of the curriculum for members of their own class **Consider how mood and atmosphere are created** in live or recorded performance	**Year 2** Read independently and with increasing fluency longer and less familiar texts **Spell with increasing accuracy and confidence,** drawing on word recognition and knowledge of word structure, and spelling patterns Know how to tackle unfamiliar words that are not completely decodable **Read and spell less common alternative graphemes** including trigraphs Read high and medium frequency words independently and automatically	**Year 2** Spell with increasing **accuracy** and confidence, drawing on word recognition and knowledge of word structure, and spelling patterns including common inflections and use of double letters **Read and spell less common alternative graphemes** including trigraphs **Understanding and interpreting texts**	**Year 2** Draw together ideas & information from across a whole text, using simple signposts in the text **Give reasons why things happen or characters change** Explain organisational features of texts, including alphabetical order, layout, diagrams etc **Use syntax & context to build their store of vocabulary** when reading **Explore how particular words are used,** including words & expressions with similar meanings	**Year 2** **Read whole books on their own,** choosing and justifying selections Engage with books through exploring and enacting interpretations **Explain their reactions to texts,** commenting on important aspects	**Year 2** Draw on knowledge and experience of texts in deciding and planning what and how to write **Sustain form in narrative,** including use of person and time Maintain consistency in non-narrative, including purpose and tense **Make adventurous word and language choices** appropriate to the style and purpose of the text Select from different presentational features to suit particular writing purposes on paper and on screen	**Year 2** Use planning to establish clear sections for writing Use appropriate language to make sections hang together	**Year 2** Write simple and compound sentences and begin to use subordination in relation to time and reason **Compose sentences using tense consistently** (present and past) Use question marks, and use commas to separate items in a list	**Year 2** Write legibly, using upper and lower case letters appropriately within words, and observing correct spacing within and between words Form and use the four basic handwriting joins **Word process short narrative and non-narrative texts**

NC KS1 Programme of Study - Literacy

(revised Framework objectives)

Numeracy 1 using and applying mathematics	Numeracy 2 counting & understanding number	Numeracy 3 knowing & using number facts	Numeracy 4 calculating	Numeracy 5 understanding shape	Numeracy 6 measuring	Numeracy 7 handling data
Year 1 **Solve problems** involving counting, adding, subtracting, doubling or halving in the context of numbers, measures or money, for example to 'pay' and 'give change' **Describe a puzzle or problem** using numbers, practical materials and diagrams; use these to solve the problem, set the solution in the original context **Answer a question** by selecting and using suitable equipment, and sorting information, shapes or objects; display results using tables and pictures **Describe simple patterns** and relationships involving numbers or shapes; decide whether examples satisfy given conditions **Describe ways of solving puzzles** and problems, explaining choices and decisions orally or using pictures	**Year 1** **Count reliably** at least 20 objects, recognising that when rearranged the number of objects stays the same; estimate a number of objects that can be checked by counting **Compare and order numbers,** using the related vocabulary; use the equals (=) sign **Read and write numerals from 0 to 20,** then beyond; use knowledge of place value to position these numbers on a number track and number line **Say the number that is 1 more or less than any given number,** & 10 more or less for multiples of 10 **Use the vocabulary of halves and quarters** in context	**Year 1** **Derive and recall all pairs of numbers with a total of 10** and addition facts for totals to at least 5; work out the corresponding subtraction facts **Count on or back in ones, twos, fives and tens** and use this knowledge to derive the multiples of 2, 5 and 10 to the tenth multiple **Recall the doubles of all numbers to at least 10**	**Year 1** **Relate addition to counting on;** recognise that addition can be done in any order; use practical and informal written methods to support the addition of a one-digit number or a multiple of 10 to a one-digit or two- digit number **Understand subtraction as 'take away'** and find a 'difference' by counting up; use practical and informal written methods to support the subtraction of a one-digit number from a one-digit or two-digit number and a multiple of 10 from a two- digit number **Use the vocabulary related to addition and subtraction and symbols** to describe and record addition and subtraction number sentences **Solve practical problems** that involve combining groups of 2, 5 or 10, or sharing into equal groups	**Year 1** **Visualise and name common 2-D shapes and 3-D solids** and describe their features; use them to make patterns, pictures and models **Identify objects that turn about a point** (e.g. scissors) or about a line (e.g. a door); recognise and make whole, half and quarter turns **Visualise and use everyday language to describe** the **position** of objects and direction and distance when moving them, for example when placing or moving objects on a game board	**Year 1** **Estimate, measure, weigh and compare objects,** choosing and using suitable uniform non-standard or standard units and measuring instruments (e.g. a lever balance, metre stick or measuring jug) **Use vocabulary related to time;** order days of the week and months; read the time to the hour and half hour	**Year 1** Answer a question by r ecording information in lists and tables; present outcomes using practical resources, pictures, block graphs or pictograms **Use diagrams to sort objects into groups** according to a given criterion; suggest a different criterion for grouping the same objects
Year 2 Solve problems involving addition, subtraction, multiplication or division in contexts of numbers, measures or pounds and pence **Identify and record the information or calculation needed to solve a puzzle or problem;** carry out the steps or calculations and check the solution in the context of the problem **Follow a line of enquiry;** answer questions by choosing and using suitable equipment and selecting, organising and presenting information in lists, tables and simple diagrams **Describe patterns and relationships** involving numbers or shapes, make predictions and test these with examples **Present solutions to puzzles and problems** in an organised way; explain decisions, methods and results in pictorial, spoken or written form, using mathematical language and number sentences	**Year 2** **Read and write two-digit and three-digit numbers in figures and words;** describe and extend number sequences and recognise odd and even numbers **Count up to 100 objects** by grouping them and counting in tens, fives or twos; explain what each digit in a two-digit number represents, including numbers where 0 is a place holder; partition two-digit numbers in different ways, including into multiples of 10 and 1 **Order two-digit numbers** and position them on a number line; use the greater than (>) and less than (<) signs **Estimate a number of objects;** round two-digit numbers to the nearest 10 Find one half, one quarter and three quarters of shapes and sets of objects	**Year 2** **Derive and recall all addition and subtraction facts for each number to at least 10,** all pairs with totals to 20 and all pairs of multiples of 10 with totals up to 100 **Understand that halving is the inverse of doubling** and derive and recall doubles of all numbers to 20, and the corresponding halves **Derive and recall multiplication facts for the 2, 5 and 10 times-tables** and the related division facts; recognise multiples of 2, 5 and 10 **Use knowledge of number facts and operations to estimate and check answers to calculations**	**Year 2** **Add or subtract mentally a one-digit number or a multiple of 10 to or from any two-digit number;** use practical and informal written methods to add and subtract two-digit numbers **Understand that subtraction is the inverse of addition and vice versa;** use this to derive and record related addition and subtraction number sentences **Represent repeated addition and arrays as multiplication,** and sharing and repeated subtraction (grouping) as division; use practical and informal written methods and related vocabulary to support multiplication and division, including calculations with remainders **Use the symbols +, -, ?, ÷ and = to record and interpret number sentences involving all four operations;** calculate the value of an unknown in a number sentence	**Year 2** Visualise common 2-D shapes and 3-D solids; identify shapes from pictures of them in different positions and orientations; sort, make and describe shapes, referring to their properties **Identify reflective symmetry in patterns and 2-D shapes** and draw lines of symmetry in shapes **Follow and give instructions involving position, direction and movement** **Recognise and use whole, half and quarter turns,** both clockwise and anticlockwise; know that a right angle represents a quarter turn	**Year 2** **Estimate, compare and measure lengths, weights and capacities,** choosing and using standard units (m, cm, kg, litre) and suitable measuring instruments **Read the numbered divisions on a scale,** and interpret the divisions between them (e.g. on a scale from 0 to 25 with intervals of 1 shown but only the divisions 0, 5, 10, 15 and 20 numbered); use a ruler to draw and measure lines to the nearest centimetre **Use units of time (seconds, minutes, hours, days) and know the relationships between them;** read the time to the quarter hour; identify time intervals, including those that cross the hour	**Year 2** Answer a question by collecting and recording data in lists and tables; represent the data as block graphs or pictograms to show results; use ICT to organise and present data **Use lists, tables and diagrams to sort objects;** explain choices using appropriate language, including 'not'

Programme of Study - Numeracy (revised Framework objectives)

SC1 scientific enquiry			SC2 life processes & living things					SC3 materials and their properties		SC4 physical processes		
Sc1.1 planning	Sc1.2 ideas & evidence; collecting evidence	Sc1.3 comparing evidence	Sc2.1 life processes	Sc2.2 humans and other animals	Sc2.3 green plants	Sc2.4 variation and classification	Sc2.5 living things in their environment	Sc3.1 grouping materials	Sc3.2 changing materials	Sc4.1 electricity	Sc4.2 forces and motion	Sc4.3 light and sound
1.1a ask questions 'How?', 'Why?', 'What if?') and decide how they might find answers to them	1.2a follow simple instructions to control the risks to themselves and to others	1.3a make simple comparisons (eg, hand span, shoe size) and identify simple patterns or associations, and try to explain it, drawing on their knowledge and understanding	2.1a differences between things that are living and things that have never been alive	2.2a recognise and compare the main external parts of the bodies of humans and other animals	2.3a recognise that plants need light and water to grow	2.4a recognise similarities and differences between themselves and others, and to treat others with sensitivity	2.5a find out about the different kinds of plants and animals in the local environment	3.1a use their senses to explore and recognise the similarities and differences between materials	3.2a find out how the shapes of objects made from some materials can be changes by some processes, including squashing, bending, twisting & stretching	4.1a about everyday appliances that use electricity	4.2a find out about, & describe the movement of, familiar things (e.g. cars going faster, slowing down, changing direction)	4.3a identify different light sources, including the Sun
1.1b use first-hand experience and simple information sources to answer questions	1.2b explore, using the senses of sight, hearing, smell, touch & taste as appropriate, & make & record observations & measurements	1.3b compare what happened with what they expected would happen, and try to explain it. Drawing on their knowledge and understanding	2.1b that animals, including humans, move, feed, grow, use their senses and reproduce	2.2b that humans and other animals need food and water to stay alive	2.3b to recognise and name the leaf, flowers, stem and root of flowering plants	2.4b group living things according to observable similarities and differences	2.5b identify similarities & differences between local environments & ways in which these affect animals & plants that are found there	3.1b sort objects into groups on the basis of their properties texture, float, hardness, transparency and whether they are magnetic or non-magnetic)	3.2b explore and describe the way some everyday materials) for example water, chocolate, bread, clay, change when they are heated or cooled	4.1b simple series circuits involving batteries, wires, bulbs and other components - eg buzzers	4.2b that both pushes and pulls are examples of forces	4.3b that darkness is the absence of light
1.1c think about what might happen before deciding what to do	1.2c communicate what happened in a variety of ways, including using ICT	1.3c review their work and explain what they did to others	2.1c relate life processes to animals and plants found in the local environment	2.2c that taking exercise and eating the right types and amounts of food help humans to keep healthy	2.3c that seeds grow into flowering plants		2.5c care for the environment	3.1c recognise and name common types of material & recognise that some of them are found naturally		4.1c how a switch can be used to break a circuit	4.2c to recognise that when things speed up, slow down or change direction, there is a cause	4.3c that there are many kinds of sound and sources of sound
1.1d Recognise when a test or comparison is unfair				2.2d about the role of drugs as medicines				3.1d find out about the uses of a variety of materials & how these are chosen for specific uses on the basis of their simple properties				4.3d that sounds travel away from sources, getting fainter as they do so, and that they are heard
			2.2e how to treat animals with care and sensitivity									
			2.2f that humans and other animals can produce offspring and that these offspring grow into adults									
			2.2g about the senses that enable humans and other animals to be aware of the world around them									

NC KS1 Programme of Study for Key Stage 1- Science

NC KS1 Programme of Study - ICT

ICT 1 — 1.1 finding things out / 1.2 developing ideas and making things happen		ICT 2 — exchanging and sharing information	ICT 3 — reviewing, modifying & evaluating work as it progresses	ICT 4 — breadth of study
1.1a gather information from a variety of sources	1.2a use text, tables, images and sound to develop their ideas	2a share their ideas by presenting information in a variety of forms	3a review what they have done to help them develop their ideas	4a work with a range of information to investigate the ways it can be presented
1.1b enter and store information in a variety of forms	1.2b select from and add to information they have	2b present their completed work effectively	3b describe the effects of their actions	4b exploring a variety of ICT tools
1.1c retrieve information that has been stored	1.2c plan & give instructions to make things happen		3c talk about what they might change in future work	4c talk about the uses of ICT inside and outside school
	1.2d try things out and explore what happens in real and imaginary instructions			

NC KS1 Programme of Study - History

H1 chronological understanding	H2 K & U of events, people & changes	H3 historical interpretation	H4 historical enquiry	H5 organisation & communication	H6 breadth of study
1a place events and objects in chronological order	2a recognise why people did things, why events happened and what happened as a result	3a identify different ways in which the past is represented	4a find out about the past from a range of sources of information	5a select from their knowledge of history and communicate it in a variety of ways	6a changes in their own lives and the way of life of their family or others around them
1b use common words and phrases relating to the passing of time (for example, before, after, a long time ago, past	2b identify differences between ways of life at different times		4b ask and answer questions about the past		6b the way of life of people in the more distant past who lived in the local area or elsewhere in Britain
					6c the lives of significant men, women and children
					6d past events from the history of Britain and the wider world

NC KS1 Programme of Study - D&T

D&T 1 developing planning & communicating ideas	D&T 2 working with tools, equipment, materials	D&T 3 evaluating processes & products	D&T 4 k & u of materials & components	D&T 5 breadth of study
1a generate ideas	2a explore sensory qualities of materials	3a talk about their ideas	4a working characteristics of materials	5a focused practical tasks
1b develop ideas	2b measure, mark out, cut and shape	3b identify improvements	4b how mechanisms can be used	5b design & make assignments
1c talk about their ideas	2c assemble, join & combine materials			5c investigate & evaluate products
1d plan what to do next	2d use simple finishing techniques			
1e communicate ideas	2e follow safe procedures			

NC KS1 Programme of Study - Geography

G1.1 & G1.2 geographical and enquiry skills		G2 knowledge & understanding of places	G3 knowledge & understanding of patterns & processes	G4 knowledge & understanding of environment	G5 breadth of study
1.1a ask geographical questions	1.2a use geographical vocabulary	2a identify and describe what places are like	3a make observations about where things are located	4a recognise changes in the environment	5a the locality of the school
1.1b observe and record	1.2b use fieldwork skills	2b identify and describe what places are	3b recognise changes in physical & human features	4b recognise how the environment may be improved & sustained	5b a contrasting locality in the UK or overseas
1.1c express their own views about people, places & environments	1.2c use globes, maps & plans at a range of scales	2c recognise how places become they way they are & how they are changing			5c study at a local scale
1.1d communicate in different ways	1.2d use secondary sources of information	2d recognise how places compare with other places			5d carry out fieldwork investigations outside the classroom
		2e recognise how places are linked to other places in the world			

Programme of Study for Key Stage 1 - Art & Design

A&D1 exploring & developing ideas	A&D2 investigating & making art, craft and design	A&D3 evaluating & developing work	A&D4 k & u of materials & components	A&D5 breadth of study
1a record from first hand observation, experience and imagination	2a investigate the possibilities of materials and processes	3a review what they and others have done	4a visual and tactile elements	5a exploring a range of starting points
1b ask and answer questions about the starting points for their work	2b try out tools and techniques and apply these	3b identify what they might change	4b materials and processes used in making art, craft and design	5b working on their own, and collaborating with others
	2c represent observations, ideas and feelings		4c differences & similarities in the work of artists, craftspeople & designers	5c using a range of materials and processes
				5d investigating different kinds of art, craft and design

Programme of Study for Key Stage 1 - Music

M1 performing skills	M2 composing skills	M3 responding & reviewing (appraising skills)	M4 responding & reviewing (listening skills)	M5 breadth of study
1a use their voices expressively by singing songs, chants, rhymes	2a create musical patterns	3a explore and express their ideas and feelings about music	4a listen with concentration & internalise & recall sounds	5a a range of musical activities
1b play tuned and untuned instruments	2b explore, choose & organise sounds & musical ideas	3b make improvements to their own work	4b how combined musical elements can be organised	5b responding to a range of starting points
1c rehearse and perform with others			4c how sounds can be made in different ways	5c working on their own, in groups and as a class
				5d a range of live and recorded music

Programme of Study for Key Stage 1 - PE

PE1 acquiring and developing skills	PE2 selecting and applying skills, tactics and compositional ideas	PE3 evaluating and improving performance	PE4 knowledge and understanding of fitness and health	PE5 breadth of study
1a explore basic skills, actions and ideas with increasing understanding	2a explore how to choose and apply skills and actions in sequence & in combination	3a describe what they have done	4a how important it is to be active	5a dance
1b remember & repeat simple skills & actions with increasing control	2b vary the way they perform skills by using simple tactics and movement phrases	3b observe, describe and copy what others have done	4b recognise & describe how their bodies feel during different activities	5b games
	2c apply rules and conventions for different activities	3c use what they have learnt to improve the quality and control of their work		5c gymnastics

Programme of Study for Key Stage 1 - PSHE

PSHEC1 developing confidence and responsibility and making the most of their abilities	PSHEC2 preparing to play an active role as citizens	PSHEC3 developing a healthier lifestyle	PSHEC4 developing good relationships & respecting differences
1a recognise their likes & dislikes, what is fair & unfair, what is right & wrong	2a take part in discussions with one other person and the whole class	3a make simple choices that improve their health & wellbeing	4a recognise how their behaviour affects other people
1b share their opinions on things that matter to them and their views	2b take part in a simple debate about topical issues	3b maintain personal hygiene	4b listen to other people and play and work co-operatively
1c recognise, name and deal with their feelings in a positive way	2c recognise choices they make, & the difference between right & wrong	3c how some diseases spread and can be controlled	4c identify and respect differences and similarities between people
1d think about themselves, learn from their experiences and recognise what they are good at	2d realise that people and other living things have needs, & that they have responsibilities to meet them	3d about the process of growing from young to old and how people's needs change	4d that family and friends should care for each other
1e how to set simple goals	2e that they belong to various groups & communities, such as a family	3e the names of the main parts of the body	4e that there are different types of teasing & bullying, that bullying is wrong
	2f what improves & harms their local, natural & built environments	3f that household products and medicines, can be harmful	
	2g contribute to the life of the class and school	3g rules for, and ways of, keeping safe, basic road safety	
	2h realise that money comes from different sources		

Credits and references

The following organisations and individuals have kindly given permission for photographs to be used in this book:
ASCO Educational

Web sites included in this book (in alphabetical order):

www.allotments-uk.com/links/gardening for kids the allotment site

www.amazon.co.uk for Underwater Sculpting Sand, an amazing and unusual sort of sand which clings together for moulding underwater, but returns to its former state immediately on removal from the water

www.applegategardens.co.uk look at 'garden design' for lots of lovely ideas for different sorts of gardens

http.arachnophiliac.co.uk for spiders, snakes and other animals that live underground

www.ascoeducational.co.uk ASCO Educational; suppliers of equipment and tools for sand play, sand trays, scoops and tools, collections of insects and frogs, a collection of woodland animals; sand combs and trays; and a set of City Blocks - wooden models of houses and other buildings

www.bbc.co.uk/gardening/design has lots of designs by TV garden designers

www.bbc.co.uk/gardening/gardening with children lots of ideas, projects, things to do

www.bgs.ac.uk The British Geological Survey site has geological maps and photos

www.buildingcentre.org.uk The Building Centre

www.cat.com Caterpillar Construction Machines click through to the shop for die cast construction models.

www.caving.uk.com is a site for cavers

www.cheddarcaves.co.uk for information about the caves in Cheddar Gorge

www.crafty-devils.com for a good range of colours in shaker bottles at a reasonable price

www.crazysand.co.uk for sand in lots of colours, bottles and gems to hide

www.deltasand.com for Delta Sand, a mouldable sort of sand and some finished projects.

www.diggerland.com is an adventure park where children can ride and drive diggers.

www.earth.google.com an aerial site for seeing everywhere, but a bit difficult to use

www.eduzone.co.uk Eduzone for sand equipment and small world toys

www.elc.co.uk Early Learning Centre for baby wild animals, dinosaur models of various sizes and farm animals.

www.emporiumuk.biz have a massive range of glass beads, marbles and other decorative beads.

www.essexminiatures.co.uk where you can click on individual models of Romans and Ancient Britons

www.gardendesigner.com where you can view and download free designs

www.gardenorganic.org.uk/schools organic network/index a good site with ideas, curriculum links, activities etc, which might help with designing a garden

www.gardenplans.com has hundreds of garden plans to look at and download

www.goodies-dollshouse-miniatures.co.uk has a new photo of a miniature every week

www.growingtreetoys.com for beach and sand toys including diggers and a ride on digger

www.gltc.co.uk (Great Little Trading Company) for Garage Town, Pirate Island, Metropolis Train sets

www.hope-education.co.uk Hope Educational Suppliers

www.hyundai.be/news/products/big-float-prefers-hyundai to look at diggers that float

www.kathimitchell.com the very best site about caves for teachers and children - click on 'caves' in the science section on the right of the page - it has lots of links to other sites about caves, cave animals, make your own stalactites, cave terms, photos, screen savers etc - you could spend a whole term here, using the links and information

www.lakeland.co.uk. Lakeland Plastics for cookware

www.ltl.org.uk Learning Through Landscapes - is an inspiring charitable organisation which will help with information on all aspects of the outdoors

www.lego.com the Lego website for variety and inspiration; consortium groups can often offer group Lego and other sets with huge numbers of pieces

www.maps.google.co.uk will give you maps of anywhere by postcode, address, street name or locality

www.multimap.com and click on aerial photos for some free examples to look at

www.museumofminiatures.org for dolls houses

www.ordnancesurvey.co.uk maps of the UK

www.outlandstone.co.uk sell stones and pebbles in lovely colours, but you have to buy at least 25kg of each or share a bag!

www.philipandtacey.co.uk have a dazzling collection of sequins, beads, glass beads, googly eyes and other objects to hide in or mix with sand; Active World Mats - which are Builders' trays with sets of characters for small world imaginative play

www.playmobil.com Playmobil have themed characters and a great range of fantasy settings, vehicles and accessories which are firm favourites of all children

www.rhs.org.uk/advice/design/design2 for pictures of the Chelsea Flower Show

www.rista.co.uk gravel, coloured sand and aggregates (not fine sand)

www.sandlady.co.uk all sorts of sand bottles and coloured sand

www.soton.ac.uk for pictures of the Isle of Wight and Alum Bay

www.stacey.peak-media.co.uk/IoW/IsleofWight for pictures of erosion of sand cliffs

www.streetmap.co.uk aerial photos

www.thekidzpage.com has free clipart

www.tiscali.co.uk/travel/maps/aerialphotos click on 'aerial photos' and put in a post code

www.toyandmodel.com/britains Britains have a huge range of www.ltl.org.uk Learning Through Landscapes farm animals in families, farm vehicles, tractors and farm people; they also make miniature fences, hay bales, animal shelters and other farm miniatures which will last for ever

www.toypost.co.uk for a Little Wooden Village and Little Wooden Farm

www.tts-group.co.uk TTS Group have a wide range of diggers and other sand toys, sieves and funnels and builder's trays; they also stock a bamboo water channelling kit which could be used for sand too, and builders' trays

www.virtualquarry.co.uk this site needs a media player to look at a quarry at work

www.ukaerialphotos.com click on Gallery for some example images of theme parks, bridges, sports stadiums etc

www.webbaviation.co.uk for county by county aerial photos

www.whitescarcave.co.uk has a good virtual tour of the caves

www.wightonline.co.uk/alumbayglass the site of a glass manufacture on the isle of Wight

www.wikipedia.org to get reference material and pictures of just about anything

www.wildgoose.ac have aerial photos, maps and a range of other geographical resources.

www.wookey.co.uk the site for Wookey Hole Caves, with photos

www.worsleyschool.net for their pictures of huge excavators

www.yellow-door.net traditional story characters, scenes and other story telling resources from Yellow Door

NB
These websites and addresses are correct at the time of printing. Please let us know if you find other interesting sources or contacts sally@featherstone.uk.com.

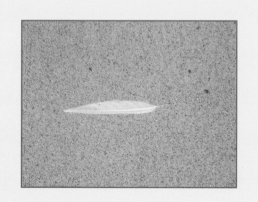

Carrying on in Key Stage One

Other titles in this series include:

Construction

Water

Role Play

Outdoor Play

Sculpting, Stuffing and Squeezing

www.acblack.com/featherstone

The EYFS – Birth to Three

Little Baby Books offer lots of ideas for working with young children, and match the original birth to three framework.

A Strong Child — A Skilful Communicator — **A Competent Learner** — A Healthy Child

Set 1
978-1-905019-21-2

Set 2
978-1-905019-22-9

Set 3
978-1-905019-23-6

Set 4
978-1-905019-24-3

Also available with the activities grouped according to stage.

Book 1 Heads-up Lookers & Communicators (124pp)
978-1-905019-50-2

Book 2 Sitters, Standers & Explorers (156pp)
978-1-905019-51-9

Book 3 Movers, Shakers & Players (172pp)
978-1-905019-52-6

Book 4 Walkers, Talkers & Pretenders (238pp)
978-1-905019-53-3

> All the activities in these books are suitable for the EYFS. Just look for the component and age you need.

Heads-up Lookers & Communicators
Stage 1: 0-8 months

Sitters, Standers & Explorers
Stage 2: 8-18 months

Movers, Shakers & Players
Stage 3: 18-24 months

Walkers, Talkers & Pretenders
Stage 4: 24-36 months

Foundations Activity Packs

Ages 3–5

Each pack: • pbk, resources & CD £24.99 • 305 x 225 mm
• 48pp • colour photographs, black and white illustrations

These award-winning activity packs are bursting with resources – ideal for all adults working with children aged 3–5.

Written by Early Years practitioners and experts.

"Everything you need to plan, organise and lead activities on early years themes"
Montessori International

The resources in each pack include:
- 50+ easy-to-follow activities
- 14 photocopiable activity sheets
- 8 colour photocards
- CD of poems, songs and stories
- Giant themed display poster
- Planning chart

Celebrations
Kate Tucker
9780713668452

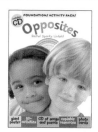
Opposites
Rachel Sparks Linfield
9780713662191

My School Day
Ann Montague-Smith
9780713661583

Minibeasts
Christine Moorcroft
9780713662184

Playsongs

9780713669404

Livelytime Playsongs
Sheena Roberts & Rachel Fuller
Early Years practitioner/ parent resource:
- £9.99
- pbk (32pp) + CD

Baby's active day in songs and pictures.
A picture songbook which tells the story of a baby's day in glorious full colour and in songs with clearly described actions. Dances, peekaboo, finger and toeplays, teasers, knee bouncers and lullabies. 0–3 years

9780713669411

Sleepytime Playsongs
Sheena Roberts & Rachel Fuller
Early Years practitioner/ parent resource:
- £9.99
- pbk (32pp) + CD

Baby's restful day in songs and pictures.
A picture songbook and CD which tells the story of baby's restful day in glorious full colour and in songs with clearly described actions. 0–3 years

9780713663716

Playsongs
Early Years practitioner/ parent resource:
- £12.99
- pbk (48pp) + CD

72 songs and rhymes for babies and toddlers.
The perfect musical start for the very young – fully illustrated book and CD. 0–3 years

To see our full range of books visit www.acblack.com

Continuity and progression through the EYFS

The Baby & Beyond series takes simple activities or resources and shows how they can be used with children at each of the EYFS development stages, from birth to 60+ months. Each double page spread covers one activity, so you can see the progression at a glance.

Ideal to support progression and extend learning.

Shows how simple resources can be used by children at different ages and stages

Inspiration for planning continuous provision

To see our full range of books visit www.acblack.com